CONTENTS

Preface and acknowledgements

This collection of papers arose out of a seminar series held at Warwick University during the academic year 1991-92. The series was funded by the Kellmer Pringle Foundation, for which all participants, and myself especially, as a Kellmer Pringle Fellow for that year, are especially grateful.

The seminar series offered us the opportunity to join with colleagues from outside and across the University, and to invite participants from further afield, so that we might explore aspects of our own and others' roles in the protection of children from abuse. We were, and still are, particularly interested in non-oppressive practice; research and theory, and how this may inform practice; ideas about potential ways forward in the education and training, and in the management, of those who work in the field, to protect children now and to prevent future child abuse and neglect.

There are many people whose support, help, and ideas have contributed to the collection and to whom I am most grateful:- the Trustees of the Kellmer Pringle Foundation; all the contributors; colleagues and students who took part in the seminar discussions; Margaret Handy, Sandra Dowse and Mary Graham, of Warwick University Education Department, for secretarial assistance; Professor Eggleston and the staff of Trentham Books, for their patience and professionalism. Thanks must also be expressed to the families and friends of contributors, whose influence is self-evident in the caring, positive attitudes and work of my collaborators, and to my own family and friends, with love.

Tricia David, Warwick University June 1993

Contributors

Su Beech has been a social worker for twenty years, initially in a London Borough and for the last five and a half years with the NSPCC, specialising in direct work with families. She is currently on the second year of a post-graduate course 'Individual work with children and young people and their families in varied settings — a Psychodynamic approach'.

Dorit Braun has worked in adult education, and then been involved in a number of curriculum development initiatives locally and nationally, focusing on issues around young children and parenting. She compiled CEDC's training guide 'Responding to Child Abuse', and has organised and delivered Child Protection training for teachers and early years workers. She is currently CEDC's Assistant Director (Development). (CEDC is the Community Education Development Centre, which is based in Coventry).

Following twenty years' experience in teaching and voluntary work with children and adults of all ages, including headships in three schools, **Tricia David** joined the Education Department at the University of Warwick, where she is a Senior Lecturer. She developed Warwick's multi-professional Early Childhood Studies Diploma course, which pre-dates the Children Act 1989 but is based on the same principles as the Act. Her research interests lie in child protection, children's rights, and multi- professionalism, and her publications include *Child Protection and Early Years Teachers* (Open University Press 1993).

Rosalind Goodyear lectures in the Education Department at Warwick University, where she teaches and develops courses in early years and primary Initial Teacher Education. Her research and publication interests lie in the areas of assessment and education policy in relation to early years and primary schooling, and in the in-service education of teachers.

After nearly twenty years of teaching and research in both Britain and Australia, **Carrie Herbert** decided to set up her own educational consultancy in Cambridge. She specialises in equal opportunities, with the emphasis on sexual harassment, and child protection and abuse prevention. Her two books are *Talking of Silence: the Sexual Harassment of Schoolgirls* and *Sexual Harassment in Schools: a Guide for Teachers*.

Adèle Jones has worked mainly in the social services sector. Her work has included: people with disabilities, problems relating to old age, child abuse, mental health, and working extensively with young people in the community. Her current role, as Social Work Consultant, involves developing anti-racist social/community work practice, also developing services that are anti-discriminatory. Adèle is a member of a large number of advisory and working groups concerned with Black issues and perspectives. She is currently working with the NSPCC on developing services to Black young people who have experienced abuse or are at risk of abuse, and is also providing developmental support to a Black Young People's Resource Centre. Adèle Jones has provided training and consultancy for a variety of organisations on a range of topics including: family placement policy and practice; the Children Act; child protection; community care, and she has contributed to a number of publications around these issues.

Judith Masson, M.A. Ph.D., is Professor of Law at Warwick University. She has taught and researched in law for 18 years, specialising in the law relating to children, particularly adoption and child protection. During the passage of the Children Act 1989 she acted as legal adviser to the Voice for the Child in Care. With former colleagues at Leicester University she co-directed the Family Support Management Project, preparing materials on Part III of the Children Act 1989 for the Department of Health's programme for the implementation of the Act. She is author of a number of books on law including *Principles of Family Law* (with Stephen Cretney) and *Children Act 1989 Manual* (with Mike Morris).

Kate Morris is a Social Work Adviser with the Family Rights Group. Prior to this she was Team Manager of the Children's Team in Warwickshire. Her current role includes responsibility for particular projects and one of her main areas of work is the development, nationally, of Family Group Conferences.

Margaret Randall is a trainee child psychotherapist and a chartered clinical psychologist. She has been a member of 'The Elms Project' since its beginning, and she has been working therapeutically with adults, young people, children and their families for the past fifteen years.

Esther Saraga is a Social Science Staff Tutor at the Open University. Her ideas derive from her work for ten years with Mary MacLeod, teaching and training students and workers in the voluntary and statutory sectors, on child abuse. Together they set up the Child Abuse Studies Unit, at what was then the Polytechnic of North London, to develop a feminist approach to theory and practice on child sexual abuse.

Anne Schonveld has worked in primary and secondary schools, as a teacher and as a school counsellor, and in a voluntary organisation with young children and their families. She has been at CEDC since 1989, primarily involved in Child Protection training with teachers.

Nick Spencer is Professor of Community Child Health at the University of Warwick. This post is shared between the School of Postgraduate Medical Education and the Department of Applied Social Studies. Prior to taking up his post at Warwick, he was a Consultant Paediatrician in Sheffield. He continues in clinical practice as a Consultant Community Paediatrician in Coventry, in which capacity he sits on the Coventry Child Protection Committee.

1
Introduction: multi-professionalism — challenges and issues

Tricia David

The public outcry which followed reports of Judge Ian Starforth Hill's comments that an eight year-old girl was 'not entirely an angel herself', (Sunday Times 13.6.1993) when sentencing her eighteen-year-old abuser to a period of probation rather than imprisonment, highlighted not only the need for greater education and training of all involved in protecting children, but also the ways in which our stereotypes of a particular profession can so easily be confirmed, despite the quiet sensitivity with which others in the same profession can be carrying out their duties.

For years people have made jokes about teachers who are unable to cope with the ill-mannered behaviour of their own offspring, social workers who are neurotic, doctors who are blissfully and arrogantly unaware of the importance of any profession other than their own — the list is endless. Yet, as with all stereotypes, our friends who belong to one of these groups are always excepted from the criticism in question.

Whenever a tragedy, such as the death of Jasmine Beckford, or a controversy like the Cleveland affair has occurred, effective inter-professional liaison has often proved to have been a stumbling block. Could some of the stereotyped views, mentioned above, be partly to blame for our failure to trust and work co-operatively with representatives of a different agency? What other factors impede the ability of professionals and volunteers to fulfil their role appropriately, placing the child's interests paramount — probably a principle which led them into their current position in the first place?

When the Children Act 1989 came into force in October 1991, the Government, to quote Professor Ron Davie (personal communication), 'moved the landing strip' on those involved in child protection, by focusing on the need to support families where children might be at risk of 'significant harm', rather than the earlier categories of physical, emotional, sexual abuse and neglect. This shift demands changes in style and approaches, quite apart from other measures which have created a new administrative climate for the 'caring professions'.

The Children Act 1989 is underpinned by certain strong principles, firstly, that the child's interests are paramount. Other principles include: the child's views, wishes and feelings, and the child's background is to be taken into account in any decisions; parental responsibility is to be recognised and supported; families are considered the best and most appropriate setting for children growing up; and there should be the development of effective multi-professional work across services, whether statutory or voluntary.

Naturally, professional and voluntary workers from different backgrounds — many examples spring to mind— have had cause to interact with one another ever since the inception of their roles. In the days when I was a nursery and primary school headteacher, for example, quite apart from the many different support staff coming into the school to work with the children, or to provide meals, inspect buildings, and so on, I had reason to meet or communicate with:- lawyers and solicitors; educational and clinical psychologists; doctors; childminders and playgroup staff; local politicians; social workers; health visitors and school nurses; probation officers; community workers; home helps; students and tutors from a range of courses in education, social work and health; police officers; leaders of local religious communities; librarians; audiologists; physiotherapists; speech therapists; ...apologies to any colleagues I have missed! Additionally, and most importantly, I met parents from many different backgrounds, each of whom brought with them their own special interests, qualities and talents.

Why is working together so important and why is it so difficult for workers to communicate, co-operate and collaborate effectively, especially when one assumes each service is there to protect children and to enhance their well-being?

Here I will focus on multi-professionalism, why is it important to debate it at this time, together with the what and why of particular challenges and issues to be considered in attempting to develop more effective collaboration.

Why work together?

Quite apart from the legal requirement instituted by the Children Act 1989, the need to work together comes from considerations of the child's or the family's needs — for a coherent, rather than confused and disparate, context. Further, the assessments, or contributions to a case conference, from differing viewpoints, brings rigour to the evidence and therefore should produce a fairer evaluation of circumstances.

As far as the professionals themselves are concerned, one would expect that the involvement of others acts as a supportive network, acting to an extent as a form of relief from an overload of responsibility. Inter-professional dialogue can provide countering views at times, which will create much-needed checks and balances in situations where adults and children could easily become stereotyped as villains and victims.

Barriers to effective inter-agency work

Stevenson (1989) points out that the idea of working together appears obvious, that the high moral ground argument 'if we only understood its importance, our concern to protect children will ensure that it happens' (p.191) is too simplistic. She asserts that life and people and situations are complex. Mandated co-operation, the result of the failure of voluntary efforts, also fails, because there is often a lack of justification to those required to implement such a policy, and a lack of the resources needed. Stevenson (1989) adds that morale among workers is a key factor in their ability to work multi-professionally. Those who have suffered cut-backs, and who feel threatened and hard-pressed, are unlikely to have sufficiently high levels of motivation, energy and commitment to throw themselves into collaborative work. Even the Audit Commission (1987) demonstrated that incentives to improve collaboration in health and community care services were not only absent for many managers, but also that there were signs that disincentives operated in that context.

Stress levels are often increased, even within a service, when the number of professional contacts increases (Baker 1988) as a result of working in teams, and it is likely that this is will be even more true when the team members come from different professional backgrounds. Firstly, stress can be induced by the feeling of letting colleagues down which results from a lack of clarity about one's role, about others' expectations, and about the effects of overload. In an interprofessional context, however, there are further factors which

3

may add to this burden. Lack of time to develop working relationships, misunderstandings about the roles of other professionals, differences in status, differing philosophies underpinning practice, together with different management structures hardly make the path of multiprofessionalism a smooth one. Steinberg (1989) goes so far as to state that

> 'because good routine collaboration between people with different expertise and approaches is the exception rather than the rule, when things go visibly wrong they tend to do so on a grand scale.' (p.121)

Research on teams and what ingredients make them effective (eg. Handy and Aitken, 1986; Morley, 1990) has largely been conducted in the industrial field, rather than the 'caring sectors', but it can be usefully mined and reflected upon both inter- and intra- professionally.

The problem, of course, is that as far as child protection work involving inter-agency collaboration is concerned, it is unlikely that multi-agency 'teams' can be selected according to the types of criteria used in industrial management settings, or in fact that there will really be time to build a team in the true sense of the word, in the current situation. What one has to consider in this case, therefore, is the question of whether we are all sufficiently flexible to adapt to work in different settings and different teams, and if not, how do we develop the skills and attitudes needed?

For adults involved in multi-professional collaboration, training is needed, covering not just the aspects such as 'the role of the social worker / police officer/ etc', but must also include preparation for case conferences and other inter-agency collaboration, to allow the adults involved to 'try on' the membership of such a 'team'.

Features of agencies

The challenges facing us in understanding each other relate also to the differences in the services for which we work. The structures may differ, management styles and priorities may create tensions either within or between services; resource allocations, especially resources in terms of finance and time for training together, may be impossible to reconcile.

A further source of stress may be the fact that we do see ourselves as representing our chosen profession, and wishing to maintain the credibility of that profession or service may become bound up in, or end up taking precedence over, our desire to do our best for the child and family with whom we are all concerned. This may be especially difficult if we are in a situation where the representatives from other services already appear to be familiar with each other, and have a deeper knowledge, or higher levels of training, concerning the legal or other requirements, for example, at a case conference. Here there are training implications for all concerned, not just for the person who feels their profession is inadequately prepared. Skilled handling of the situation by whoever is co-ordinating or chairing should allay any fears of this kind and provide each member of the group with the opportunities for fulfilling their particular role.

Sharing theoretical underpinnings

In addition to the other difficulties already presented, it can be disconcerting to work with others who suddenly expose their theories about the causes of child abuse, and to find that they are at odds with one's own. The case conference is hardly the time or place to begin such a debate, yet the lack of acceptance for alternative views, or the lack of coherence, may make it impossible for those with the differing views to operate together effectively. Sue Richardson and Heather Bacon (1991) discuss the way in which such conflict must be dealt with, and that it can be used creatively to move forward in the interests of children.

> 'Conflict makes implicit beliefs explicit and it may not be possible to assess the health of a system until this happens. At this stage it can be expedient to retreat behind agency boundaries rather than be left with ownership of a problem which cannot be solved and which threatens existing social and professional hierarchies.' (p. 28)

Their argument is both sensible and powerful. It is important to recognise that such debates must be held and thus time, possibly during joint training sessions, needs to be allocated for such discussions and the resolution of conflict. However, as Tony Newton, then a minister at the DHSS, stated in 1982, there is also a need to guard against the paralysis which can occur when professionals put undue emphasis on achieving consensus (speech quoted in Jones et al, 1987). The main point is deciding what is in the best interests of the children involved, and differences in belief systems of professionals are unlikely to be changed overnight, for they will be grounded in past histories. When one considers the groups of professionals who could be involved in a case (for a very full list see Jones et al, 1987, p.52-53), at least 42 different professions from ten different agencies, it seems naive to expect that everyone will have the same views on child abuse, its causes, family life, and childhood. Further, it will be politicians who will provide the context in which all these professionals work, and it is therefore important for them to be engaged in the debate at some points, so that they are able to evaluate the needs of workers and to assess the effects of their own policies. This means more voices added to the debate and further, it is one which would benefit from community involvement.

However, Blyth and Milner (1990) raise the argument that many members of the public do not want to be engaged in the debate about child abuse; they simply want those who have been delegated the task of undertaking this 'dirty work' (protecting abused children) to get on with it silently.

The personal and the professional

The extent to which different agencies work well together has often been at the mercy of human frailty. Since the most important people, the people at the centre of the multi-professional endeavours are the children, it is wrong that this should be so. Unfortunately it is impossible to rule out human weakness, and, to counter this, there are doubtless other instances where the humans concerned gave more than 100 per cent. What we need to explore are the ways in which human frailty, (for example, lack of flexibility, or an inability to get on with a representative of another agency), can be overcome by the setting up of procedures.

Co-operation between organisations is a very complex matter, and is dependent upon the level of co-operation needed for any one task, and the extent to which each organisation is drawn into the collaborative work.

Effectiveness will also depend, crucially, upon the values, attitudes, decision-making processes, organisational integration, professional co-ordination, social position, economic strength and environmental adaptation of each group. As Payne (1982) points out, the similarity in values, and the styles of management and patterns of communication (organisational integration) will influence the ability for mutual understanding. So too will attitudes towards professional co-ordination because this will underpin action and caring styles adopted. Competent and confident in their own roles and positions in society, such professionals will be enabled to work positively together. Whether this is feasible in a climate in which most of the main groups under discussion here have been under attack over a prolonged period from central government is debatable.

When difficulties arise between professionals from different services, informal contacts based on mutual respect can provide the links which mean the problem will be seen as soluble.

Two further strategies for developing co-operation are the setting up of structures, and interchange (Payne, 1982). For example, to an extent, the Department for Education and the Department of Health have required schools to develop the structures for multi-professional collaboration through the naming of a teacher responsible for liaison, the demand for local authority guidelines and better delineation of responsibilities in child protection work (Home Office et al, 1991).

In many ways, interchange, as described by Payne (1982), joint discussions, sharing of documentation, ideas, etc, is also dealt with by the same publication, in that joint training is a recommendation. If interchange is really vital to inter-agency co-operation, then workers should use the tenets of the Children Act 1989 to bring home this point. Inter-agency training (and any other interchange) cannot happen without proper resourcing.

An ecological model — the importance of context

In exploring the practice of anyone working in the field of child protection it seems important to address both the personal and the professional, the private and the public spheres of their life and experience and, in particular, the contextual influences on their roles, responsibilities and how they 'make sense' of the world in which they have to operate (Bronfenbrenner 1979).

What is important about using an ecological model is the way in which child abuse and attitudes towards children will be seen as dependent upon the overarching ideology, as well as the political and economic climate, of a society or subculture, not simply as emanating from one person, family or community group.

Changing contexts — changing professionals or changing families?

The translation of ideological and political beliefs into policies and laws operating in the context set by the current conditions, whether national or local, is an important area for analysis by those working in the field.

For example, Parton (1991) argues that in

> 'trying to redistribute resources away from more generalised welfare provision towards law and order, and in trying to free the market and the family as the best ways of allocating resources and ensuring individual freedoms, the role of law becomes primary...The primary significance of a move towards legalism in child care is that the form of interventions will change and, perhaps more crucially, the boundaries between the private family and the state and between state agencies should, in theory, become much clearer.' (Parton 1991, p. 202).

As Parton goes on to state, such changes are taking place in a changing economic and social climate, which has had a direct influence on all services, whether statutory or voluntary. The proportion of young children and their families living in poverty has increased (Bradshaw 1990; CPAG 1988) while at the same time the Government is intent upon finding ways to cut public spending so that only certain families can be prioritised for intervention, leaving others where there may well be need for support either without the type of services they themselves might identify as appropriate, or, as Parton argues, under closer scrutiny, (for example, in family centres rather than day nurseries). It is true that less suspected child abuse cases are being brought to court, but is this the result of a reduction in abuse, better focused support, better partnership with parents, or something else?

Parton (1991) considers that the macro-context set by the New Right has created a shift in the role of child protection agencies because the emphasis has moved, firstly, from one where child abuse is a socio-medical problem, to one in which social workers still play a key role, but in conjunction with legal agencies, that is, it is now a socio-legal issue; secondly, the situation has been moved from one in which an examination of child protection practices would be central in seeking to improve the lot of children at risk, to one in which the form and nature of the family is to be delineated so that

8

'most of us must know what good childcare and good parenthood 'is' and what constitutes normal family relationships' (Parton 1991, p.214).

The UN Convention on Children's Rights, despite scepticism that even in the most affluent countries it will take some years to achieve complete fulfilment of all Articles, may well be yet another feature of the overall context in the UK and internationally which confirms this move towards a socio-legal emphasis, while at the same time it could herald many new ideas about what constitutes abuse or rather, significant harm. Child protection may come to be viewed as ensuring compliance by parents, family, the State and the UN of the Articles of the Convention. For example, at some time in the future are we going to see indoctrination into a particular religion, or being forbidden to meet certain friends, or deprivation of the family home, or suffering from the effects of a war or racism, as child protection issues, that is, as infringing of children's rights and potentiating risk of factors newly accepted as constituting significant harm?

Further, we have at our disposal a much greater fund of research information about children's development and understanding, about how children 'make sense' of the world and of their lives, than was available even twenty years ago, at least in any formal and acknowledged capacity. This has had an effect upon the way children's evidence is viewed and, importantly, upon attitudes towards decision-making and children's right to be involved. Is it because today's children and the nature of childhood have changed with the development of recognition for children as people in their own right, with their own ideas, wishes and feelings?

Those seeking to implement positive strategies for multi-professional collaboration must do so, therefore, in an atmosphere of change, change in the way services are funded and run, change in the way children and their families are to be viewed and approached. For some adults, even those who have chosen to work in the caring services, this may mean a painful attitudinal change, one which requires them to rethink their perceived role in relation to children.

It is usually thought that those who work in the caring professions with children will be committed to their best interests, and thus to what those adults may perceive as advocacy of children's rights. One cannot help but be haunted by the words of Michael King (1981), despite the fact that they predate the Children Act by almost a decade:

'The final decision within the existing legal framework will always lie with adults. Both common law and statutes are couched in deliberately vague and general terms to allow legal and administrative decision-making concerning children to reflect the perceptions of the decision-makers as to the best interests of children. The systems are paternalistic and protectionist ... Unless and until children are able to gain some access to economic and political power, it is difficult to see how their situation within the legal and welfare systems is likely to change, even if the proponents of children's rights achieve their objectives.' (p.133-4)

Members of the professional groups involved in child protection tend to come from the educated middle classes. As such, even those who do not agree with King's view must repeatedly ask themselves whether, by working together more effectively, they are indeed working in the best interests of all children, or operating as a 'club' or 'team', which maintains the status quo, ensuring the passing on of cultural capital to children in their own stratum of society, while working 'on' certain families and certain children.

Roles and responsibilities

This leads us to a consideration of role delineation in child protection. Garbarino and Stott (1989) have suggested that we each have a view of ourselves and the part we wish to play in relation to children when involved in child protection work. Despite the role we may have been designated by society, as investigator, therapist, or clinical evaluator, we may find our actual roles 'inappropriately tangled' (Garbarino and Stott 1989, p. 293), especially when demands may be made on us from more than one source. If a clinician is required to serve in court, or an investigator feels great sympathy for the child involved and fails to register some important but compromising evidence, role conflict may occur. Many observers (Bray 1993; Garbarino and Stott 1989; Wattam 1992) feel that the needs of the child are often subordinated to the needs of the legal system, even in the case of the new memorandum of *Good Practice for Interviewing Children* (Home Office 1989). We have to ask ourselves what we consider our role to be — is it that of advocate, therapist, guardian, impartial evaluator, or decision maker/judge — the roles suggested by Garbarino and Stott (1989)? There are no doubt additional roles to add to the list — for example, preventer, which is a role a social worker who supports families may wish to take up, or a teacher who decides to engage with parents and children in developing an understanding of children's rights and children's personhood (David 1993).

Certainly it would appear that the police have a clear view of themselves as upholding the law (Tuck 1993), and health visitors have worked on their perspective, because it would be all too easy for families to begin to view them as spies rather than allies who hold their children's interests paramount (Blackburn 1993). These professionals have come to a decision as to where their main responsibility lies — but if this perspective has not been shared with other professionals and volunteers with whom they are working their behaviour and contributions may be regarded with some mistrust.

One of the other aspects which will affect the role we take up will be our identity in a personal as well as a professional sense. Many of our attitudes will be derived from our earlier experiences. Our life histories will impinge on the theories we espouse, the political view we have of families and children, and of services. They will have influenced our decision to take one career path rather than another, whether or not we were selected, and our earlier education and training will have contributed to the philosophy, beliefs and practices to which we adhere. Our status in a multi-professional group may be a function of our professional background and qualifications, but it may also be influenced by others' perceptions of us in relation to gender, race, class, disability and even age, as well as to personal qualities and whether we work for a statutory or a voluntary agency.

Positive action

The new edition of *Working Together* (Home Office, DoH, DES and Welsh Office, 1991) makes a number of significant recommendations, including the need for agencies to establish joint annual training programmes, involving trainers from all the relevant agencies, and under the auspices of the ACPC.

Other strategies aimed at improving inter-agency collaboration include: the naming of a key worker as the co-ordinator; the use of evidence from both social and medical assessments; the special training of the persons who will chair case conferences; the essential nature of each school having a named person as the teacher responsible for child protection liaison work, and for ensuring on-going training for all staff; the establishment of special teams to deal with particularly complex or controversial cases of sexual abuse.

The need for training

Multi-professional training could lead to greater understanding of one another's roles and responsibilities, services and codes of conduct. It could also enable a sharing of theoretical underpinnings, although it may not be true to say that any one profession takes a particular theoretical stance. Preferred theories may tell us more about the persons espousing them than their professional background, but by bringing them into the open they may expose potential sources of conflict in a way which may help us use them profitably.

It is vital, therefore, to have other opportunities to confront our differences, in situations which allow us the time to develop trust.

What may also be needed is a careful exploration of the knowledge fields of other professions, particularly some of the most up-to-date developments, and at the same time an overview of the changes in that service. For example, many in the education service consider the 1988 Education Reform Act to be legislation which is actually contradicted by the Children Act 1989 for a number of reasons, one of which is that the parent is the 'client' with respect to the ERA, whereas the child and the child's views are central for the Children Act (David 1992).

Further, over the last decade, teachers have moved a long way in their ability to undertake assessment procedures, and their understandings of contextual influences on the way children will behave if assessment is carried out under strange conditions. They could in fact be the appropriate group to carry out observational and interview work in children's familiar settings (ie. schools), if given the training required. In other words, a careful exploration of the knowledge and skills already at our disposal in a multi-professional field might yield more efficient and effective ways of working together, by using identified skills more effectively.

Sharing information

Anxieties about passing on information which may be used in proceedings over which one has no further control can also create a climate of mistrust. Yet sharing information — networking — with experienced workers from another background, perhaps initially presenting the child's case anonymously, is a potential source of support. However, models of professional practice related to each profession's view of confidentiality and their code of conduct do need to be part of any multi-professional training if these barriers are to be overcome.

Remembering the child and the family

Although this paper has deliberately focused on the challenges and issues involved in developing multi-professionalism, the central reason for this development must not be forgotten. In other words, multi-professionalism must not become an end in itself, nor what may seem to be effective ways of working together become ways of excluding the family and working *on* children and their parents, rather than *with* them.

In this book we are presenting ideas about aspects of multi-professionalism in child protection which could promote the changes in attitude necessary for positive co-operation and collaboration. We hope too that we explore the values required by our respective professions, agencies and society in general if we are truly to protect children and prevent significant harm.

In the papers which follow, Judith Masson sets the scene with her discussion of the legal issues; Adèle Jones challenges us to promote an anti-racist underpinning to all our work, as a matter of social justice; Nick Spencer confronts the paternalistic attitudes of the medical profession and the collusion of other agency workers in this; Margaret Randall and Su Beech present an honest and moving case study of the struggle of a team seeking to develop child-centred practice; Kate Morris argues that despite the Children Act and the revised guidelines for working together, families are still excluded by the multi-agency group of professionals involved but she provides some suggestions for a way forward; Ros Goodyear, Dorit Braun and Anne Schonveld discuss the difficulties faced by teachers trying to develop child protection skills at both initial and in-service levels; Carrie Herbert debates the need for sensitivity in research and the development of appropriate research methods; and finally, Esther Saraga emphasises the need for us to come to terms with the uncertainty which pervades this field of work, but couples this with a demand that we at least become thoughtful in our search for theory which will inform both practice and the debate itself — a call which all of us who consider multi-professionalism a way to professional and academic enrichment will find irresistible, especially if it can improve the quality of life for children.

References

Audit Commission (1987) *Making a Reality of Community Care* London, HMSO

Baker, B. (1988) GPs in group practice are under more stress, *Pulse 88*, 6, p.1

Blackburn, C. (1993) 'The Role of the Health Visitor' Lecture, Warwick University, February 1993

Blyth,E. and Milner, J. (1990) 'The process of inter-agency work' in Violence Against Children Study Group (Eds) *Taking Child Abuse Seriously* London, Unwin Hyman

Bradshaw, J. (1990) *Child Poverty and Deprivation in the UK* London, National Children's Bureau

Bray, M. (1993) 'Therapeutic work with children' NANFC Conference, Peterborough, March 1993

Bronfenbrenner, U. (1979) *The Ecology of Human Development* Cambs Mass, Harvard University Press

CPAG (1988) *Child Poverty: the facts* London, Child Poverty Action Group

David, T. (Ed) (1992) *The Children Act 1989: the First Six Months* Warwick University Coventry, OMEP

David, T. (1993) *Child Protection and Early Years Teachers* Buckingham, Open University Press

Garbarino, J. and Stott, F. (1989) *What Children Can Tell Us* London, Jossey-Bass

Handy, C. and Aitken, R. (1986) *Understanding Schools as Organisations* Harmondsworth, Penguin

Home Office (1989) *Report of the Advisory Group on Video Evidence* London, HMSO

Jones, D.N., Pickett, J., Oates, M.R. and Barbor, P.R.H. (1987) *Understanding Child Abuse* London, Macmillan Educational

King, M. (1981) *Childhood, Welfare and Justice* London, Batsford

Morley, I.E. (1990) 'Building cross-functional design teams' Proceedings of the First International Conference on Integrated Design Management, p.100-110. IFS Conferences

Parton, N. (1991) *Governing the Family* London, Macmillan

Payne, M. (1982) *Working in Teams* London, Macmillan Educational/BASW

Richardson, S. and Bacon, H. (1991) *Child Sexual Abuse: whose problem?* Birmingham, Venture Press

Steinberg, D. (1989) *Interprofessional Consultation* Oxford, Basil Blackwell

Stevenson, O. (Ed) (1989) *Child Abuse: Public Policy and Professional Practice* London, Harvester-Wheatsheaf

Tuck, S. (1993) 'Report on a 'shadowing' exercise.' Unpublished work undertaken in part fulfilment of the B.Phil.(Ed) degree Warwick University

Wattam, C. (1992) *Making a Case in Child Protection* Harlow, Longman

2
Developing legal issues in child protection

Judith Masson

In the last five years there have been major developments in both the civil and criminal law relating to child protection. These developments have largely occurred without reference to one another and without consideration of how each might affect the ability of the other to protect individual child victims. This chapter seeks to examine the combined impact of those changes and to identify the resulting practice issues.

History

The first child protection statute — the Prevention of Cruelty to Children Act 1889 — allowed a court to commit the child's care to a fit person (the forerunner of the care order) only if the carer was bound over, convicted or committed for trial for ill-treating a child. The Act was amended and extended in 1894. The Prevention of Cruelty to Children (Amendment) Act 1894 concluded a list of offences — the Schedule 1 offences which could all be used to found a fit person order. It was not until 1952 that civil proceedings could be taken in cases of abuse without criminal proceedings although abandoned and neglected children might be received into care and made subject to a parental rights resolution.

Despite the creation of a separate civil jurisdiction based on the concepts of ill-treatment and neglect, Schedule 1 offences have remained important in child protection. The Schedule 1 offender is a symbol of evil and dangerousness, abusers are identified as such (sometimes inaccurately because there has been no conviction) by workers who could not find the Schedule nor state which offences are included. Complex mechanisms have been established to ensure

15

that those employed to care for children have not committed offences against them (DH, 1992)

The civil jurisdiction was necessary because, despite some changes in the rules of evidence, prosecutions were very difficult. Children were only regarded as competent witnesses if they understood the nature of the oath — in practice they had to be about 8 years old — and their evidence had to be corroborated. A procedure was introduced in 1894 which allowed children to give evidence by a written deposition to a JP if a doctor certified that giving evidence would involve serious danger to health or life but was rarely used. The English courts were wedded to the idea that justice could only be done if evidence was oral. (Spencer and Flin, 1990)

After 1933 the civil system developed independently. Prosecutions were used as the basis for some care proceedings — where there was a conviction for a Schedule 1 offence this could shorten the civil case, but parallel prosecutions were frequently seen as a factor which delayed the civil case despite guidance which aimed to prevent this (Home Office Circular 84/1982). The Children Act 1989 completed the separation of two processes by ending the commission of a Schedule 1 offence as grounds for a care order. Now it is necessary to prove actual or likely significant harm in all cases (Children Act 1989, s.31). Evidence of a conviction could form the basis of this but it is not sufficient in itself (Masson, 1990). It is not necessary to wait for the completion of the criminal trial — there is provision which gives witnesses indemnity against self incrimination and thus encourages admissions in civil proceedings (Children Act 1989, s.98).

Criminal Law

Although until recently criminal lawyers largely expressed contentment with the English criminal justice system, they were not proud of the way it failed to deal adequately with offences against children. Indeed it came to be regarded as something of a disgrace (Spencer, 1987). The main problems relate to children as witnesses — competence and corroboration, also the need to give evidence orally and be cross-examined. These problems, as we will see, have been tackled (but not necessarily solved) by the Criminal Justice Acts 1988 and 1991. There are further problems which also affect children, relating to the role of the victim in the prosecution process and the length of time between the offender's arrest and the case being completed. There were also some, including Louis Blom-Cooper (prominent because of his chairing of two Inquiries into child deaths), who viewed intra-family child abusers as victims who needed help. They rejected the use of prosecution but ignored the possible adverse consequences of decriminalisation. Such an approach may only serve to reinforce the attitudes of perpetrators that they have done no wrong, and sits ill with changes in the approach to violence and sex offences against wives which have brought active policing against domestic violence and recognition of rape in marriage as a criminal offence (Viinikka, 1989).

The combined effect of the 1988 and 1991 Acts is to enable children who are able to give a coherent account of their abuse to be witnesses in criminal proceedings. Children will give their evidence in chief in the form of a pre-recorded video, made as early as possible in the investigation but will have to be available for cross-examination at the trial (Criminal Justice Act 1991, s.54). Cross-examination will usually take place using the live-link video system introduced in 1988. The accused will not be able to cross-examine the child in person nor will there be two trials, because committal proceedings will not be required in these cases. Children's evidence no longer has to be corroborated but the warning of the dangers of convicting on uncorroborated evidence must still be given in cases of sexual offences. These changes remove some of the barriers against prosecution but may not make it easier to obtain a conviction. A Memorandum of Good Practice has been drafted with the aim of ensuring that pre-trial videos can be admitted — ensuring that interviewers do not lead the child or ask questions which produce inadmissible hearsay (Home Office, 1992). Videos will be shown to the accused before the trial with the aim of inducing a guilty plea. Where this does not occur there are likely to be attempts to have it excluded and conduct vigorous cross-examination of the child. Cross-examination is the most problematic aspect of giving evidence for child abuse victims — it is frequently confrontational and often involves accusations that the child is lying (Davis and Noon, 1991). Not only are these upsetting and so might prevent a child being able to complete his or her evidence, they also make real the abuser's threat that the child will not be believed.

Sentencing

Guilty pleas, if they truly amount to acceptance of responsibility for the offence, may help the victim not only by sparing her from the trauma of cross examination but also by removing the guilt she may feel for what has occurred. However, the criminal justice system is not designed to elicit such pleas — indeed concern about false confessions makes further pressure on defendants likely to be viewed as dangerous and unjust. Glaser and Spencer have argued that the current sentencing policy outlined in the Attorney General's references discourages guilty pleas because even having given one the accused is unlikely to be spared a prison sentence (Glaser and Spencer, 1990).

Butler-Sloss has argued that consideration should be given to diversion programmes for abusers who are willing to subject themselves to control (Butler-Sloss, 1988). Cautioning is available provided there is sufficient evidence for a prosecution, if the offender admits his guilt and he agrees to be cautioned. Home Office statistics indicate that cautioning for sexual offenders is rare except where the perpetrator is under 21, when it is the most common response (Home Office, 1991). Butler-Sloss's concern comes from her focus on the child and the view that prosecution even after a guilty plea may do further damage to the child. The child may blame herself, and be blamed by the family for the father's imprisonment and the consequential hardship suffered. Unfortunately, evidence from the United States does not hold out much hope for the diversionary approach. Offenders rarely seek help unless confronted with a strong chance of imprisonment; coerced participation in programmes does not indicate acceptance of responsibility nor willingness to change; and there is little evidence of the ability of treatment programmes to provide a cure and thus protect children in the future (Horton, 1990).

Prison removes the opportunity to commit offences against children (but not the opportunity to victimise other adults or to fantasise about sexual relations with children). There are fears that rather than discouraging reoffending, it increases such behaviour (Murray and Gough, 1991). Sexual offenders are victimised by other prisoners and thus seek refuge in rule 43, which places them with other sexual offenders, or in an alternative criminal record. Either way the offending behaviour remains unchallenged and the problems which produced it are not addressed.

Concerns about the appropriateness of prosecution arise not only from the difficulty of obtaining a conviction and the effects of imprisonment on the offender but also from the process of investigation and the decision to prosecute.

Investigation

Investigations in child sexual abuse cases start in a variety of different ways. Children may make clear disclosures of recent abuse, be physically examined providing samples which will give forensic evidence and directly identify the perpetrator, but such cases are extremely rare. It is more likely that there will have been concerns about the child's case for sometime — sexually abused children are often physically abused and neglected — and disclosures of abuse are more likely to be made when the child feels safe from the perpetrator, perhaps because he has left the family or she has gone into foster care (La Fontaine, 1990). If allegations do not 'come out of the blue' but following social services involvement the emphasis in the Children Act 1989 on partnership should mean that social services has sought to establish trusting relationships with the parents and the child. Sensitive handling of any investigation is essential. Two specific issues (involving the parents in the case conference and preparing the video of the child's statement) have to be addressed. Handling these inappropriately may make it more difficult to protect the child by maintaining her trust, to establish a working relationship for protection with the mother or another non-abusing family member, and can also undermine future legal proceedings. Decisions will have to be made with foresight not with hindsight and under pressure from other agencies. Although criminal prosecutions are still likely to occur in only a small percentage of cases, there is a danger that the demands of the criminal courts will dominate because it will not be possible to determine at this early stage which cases could and should proceed to the criminal courts.

Parents at case conferences

Partnership would seem to demand involvement in decision making and shared aims. Although this may not be possible with both parents at the early stages of an investigation, June Thoburn argues that keeping them fully informed and involving them as much as possible is more likely to produce partnership as the case progresses (Thoburn, 1991). She makes a strong case for parents attending the whole of a case conference and for practices which indicate to parents that their attendance is valuable (Thoburn, 1992). She dismisses concerns particularly from local authority lawyers that parents may be disadvantaged because they may incriminate themselves (or that statements they make cannot be used in a criminal trial because they have not been cautioned) on the basis that very few prosecutions will occur. This however may not be a sufficient response. For individual parents there may be fear of prosecution which discourages them from attending or speaking. Parental ignorance of this risk cannot be a good basis for a partnership. It might be better if case conferences were privileged so that statements made in them could not be used in criminal trials. The police would be able to interview parents after the conference and they would be free as others are to refuse to answer questions. Statements would remain available as admissible hearsay in care proceedings as they are at present (Children Act 1989, s.96).

Interviewing the child

This is perhaps more problematic. Recent childcare practice has sought to prevent the revictimization of the victim by developing 'child centred' practice which is aimed at empowering the victim (Richardson and Bacon, 1991). The Children Act 1989 has taken this approach by enabling mature young people to decide not to submit to examinations or assessments even though the effect of this is to undermine the care case which could give them some protection. However, practice must keep a balance between giving responsibility to children and making them responsible for the decision taken. Adults will inevitably retain more power than children since children's information and choices are limited by adults. The option most children would choose — an unbroken home with no abuse — as if it had never happened — is not available and there are severe limits on the professional's chances of even getting near to this ideal.

As a victim of a criminal offence the child has little say in the way the case is investigated (Morgan and Zedner, 1992). The Memorandum of Good Practice on video recording identifies the issue of the child's needs but only addresses the child's developmental needs in terms of her ability to provide a coherent and credible account on video in response to questions. 'Needs' thus relate to the way the interview is conducted rather than participating in the decision to pursue the case in this way. Moreover the child is a compellable witness and so could be ordered to attend court. The Memorandum of Good Practice makes it clear that the Crown Prosecution Service should take into account the child's wishes — this information should be, but is not always, provided to them (Wattam 1992). However in a criminal matter the child's wishes cannot be decisive. Compellability is likely to infect the approach to video recording, not by coercing responses since these would be useless in a trial, but by

20

creating an expectation that a recording will be made. The recording becomes something for which the professionals must prepare, which will happen to the child because this is the way cases are processed, just as the Cleveland children were subject to medical examination although, hopefully, without the repetitions.

The way the videoed interview is conducted must also be of concern. The Memorandum of Good Practice recommends following its stepwise approach in all cases because it will be carried out before it is clear whether there will be a prosecution. The interview is clearly investigative not therapeutic, although it has been suggested (somewhat hopefully) that once it is 'in the can' the child can go into therapy without the fear that her evidence might be contaminated (Cobley, 1992). The agenda for the interview has to be set by the interviewer who will have to try and keep the child on track. The child will not normally be accompanied for fear of contamination of her evidence but may be allowed an appropriate adult if she requests it. Given this advice interviewers may not offer a supporter. The interview must go at the child's pace but should normally last less than an hour and should be completed in a single day. Given these limitations there will be considerable pressure on the interviewer to get it done quickly and to press on with the interview rather than talk about the child's concerns.

The video will be used in civil and criminal proceedings and recordings may be sought by the defence as well as the prosecution. Cases with some other evidence, perhaps a confession by an abuser which is retracted, may be undermined if the child's recording does not produce the necessary evidence. In civil proceedings, videos may be used instead of the interviewer's indirect evidence which is admissible hearsay under the Children Act 1989. The civil courts are also likely to expect interviewers to follow the Memorandum and be less willing to accept as adequate evidence other recordings or indirect statements. There is also a danger that the trend to expect high levels of proof in sex abuse cases in wardship (Re G. (a minor) (1988) 1FLR 314; Lyon and de Cruz, 1990) will be reflected in expecting a videoed statement in civil proceedings which would satisfy the criminal courts at least in cases involving older children.

The decision to prosecute
The decision to prosecute remains with the CPS and is largely based on an examination of the evidence although issues of public interest are considered (Director of Public Prosecutions, 1985). Despite the

'Victim's Charter the victim remains out of the focus of the criminal law:'The police and the CPS are bound to consider the case from a different viewpoint from the victim' (Home Office, 1990). This may lead them to prosecute against the victim's wishes (more usually in adult cases to drop a case the victim or her family would like pursued) or to charge with a less serious offence because this facilitates conviction. In these cases, as in civil cases, there may be no right answer but there is a need to raise the confidence of families, professionals and the public in the decision reached by the CPS. A report from the police about the child's wishes with the video is not an adequate basis for exercising the discretion to prosecute. Rather the issues of prosecution or caution should be fully discussed at an inter-professional meeting which would make a recommendation, with reasons, to the CPS. Professionals working with the child may be in a better position to judge the child's response to cross examination and can provide further information about the likely impact of conviction on the child and the family. These matters should be fully considered when the decision to prosecute is made. Once the decision to prosecute has been made, a firm timetable should be set for the trial because of the trauma that delay places on the child and her current carers (Viinikka, 1989).

Others who have written about the changes in the criminal law expect them to increase prosecution and conviction rates both of which have fallen markedly in recent years (Cobley, 1992; Home Office, 1989; Fotheringham et al, 1991). This they see as beneficial — so that we can be said to be 'approaching the stage where the prosecution of child abusers can be actively encouraged by all concerned' (Cobley, 1992). I remain more sceptical. I am concerned that the return to the criminal law will undermine the protection that civil proceedings and the Children Act context of partnership can give. Also that whilst the criminal law largely ignores the victim it will continue to undermine the adoption of child centred practice. This is not to advocate decriminalisation but to be aware that the welfare of the individual victim may in some cases be better served by procedures and practices designed to support her and maintain her family or the remnants of it. Changing the rules of evidence in ways which *may* make prosecution easier in some cases but could undermine civil proceedings cannot be guaranteed to do that.

Conclusion

Child protection law has two distinct aims — to safeguard and promote the welfare of the child and to prevent the abuse of other children in the community. These aims may not always be consistent. Recent developments may have increased the cases where they are in conflict. The Children Act 1989 has changed the focus of the civil system from rescue ideology to the idea of meeting children's needs whenever possible within the family and without court proceedings. In general although cautioning offenders and treatment rather than punishment are theoretically possible, these approaches remain poorly developed in relation to those who commit offences against children. Such approaches are still likely to be viewed as inappropriate because they do not sufficiently indicate society's abhorrence of child abuse.

Prosecution of the perpetrator for a Schedule 1 offence still has benefits for the community: it usually leads to imprisonment which temporarily *protects* the community; *labelling* the perpetrator as a Schedule 1 offender may assist tracing his whereabouts after release and prevent further abuse through the system of police checks on those whose occupations give them access to children. However, prosecution of the perpetrator may have adverse consequences for the individual child victim. The outcome of abuse is least bad for victims of perpetrators who accept responsibility for their actions and victims who are believed and supported by their mothers (La Fontaine, 1990; Conte and Shuerman, 1987). Prosecution may undermine both these. Failed prosecution has disastrous effects: the perpetrator's threat that the child will not be believed comes true; civil proceedings may be made more difficult and the child can be left without protection or the belief that help will come.

It is no longer possible to face these dilemmas by ignoring the criminal justice system on the basis that the rules of evidence prevent the realistic possibility of conviction in almost every case. Changes in the Criminal Justice Acts 1988 and 1991 make it easier for children's evidence to be heard but will not necessarily increase the proportion of perpetrators who acknowledge their guilt. They will not make children more credible to juries nor protect them from the traumas of waiting for trial or being cross examined. However, they will re-focus all investigations of sexual abuse and place a high premium (and consequent stress) on the ability of professionals to conduct investigative interviews appropriately. There is a danger that in the needs of the video those of the child will be lost.

The changes in criminal procedure and evidence make it essential that there is an open debate about the appropriateness of prosecution generally; that treatment strategies are fully evaluated and successful ones made available to those likely to benefit; and that systems are developed to ensure the best decisions in individual cases. The responsibility for prosecution may be that of the state but the community should not be asked to endorse approaches which place identified victims at risk of further harm where the benefits to unidentified ones cannot be demonstrated.

References

Blom-Cooper, L. (1985) *A Child in trust — report of the Inquiry into the death of Jasmine Beckford*, L.B. Brent.

Blom-Cooper, L. (1987) *A child in mind — report of the Inquiry into the death of Kimberley Carlisle*, L.B. Greenwich.

Butler-Sloss, E. (1988) *Report of the Committee of Inquiry into child abuse in Cleveland* (1988) Cm 412.

Cobley, C. (1992) Child abuse, child protection and the criminal law, 4.J. *Child Law*, 78.

Conte, J. and Shuerman, J. (1987) Factors associated with an increased impact of child sexual abuse, 11 *Child Abuse and Neglect*, 201-211.

Department of Health (1992) *Choosing with care*, (The Warner Report) HMSO.

Davis, G. and Noon, E. (1991) *An evaluation of the live link for child witnesses*, Home Office.

Director of Public Prosecutions (1985) Code for Crown Prosecutors.

Fotheringham, T. et.al. (1991) Child sexual abuse: diagnosis and working together before and after Cleveland. Paper presented at BASPCAN Conference, Leicester University 1991.

Glaser, D. and Spencer, J. (1990) Sentencing, children's evidence and children's trauma (1990) *Criminal Law Review*, 371.

Home Office, (1989) *Report of the Advisory Groups on Video evidence*, Home Office.

Home Office (1990) *The Victim's Charter*, Home Office.

Home Office (1992) *Memorandum of good practice on video recorded interview with child witnesses for criminal proceedings*, HMSO.

Home Office (1991) *Criminal Statistics*, 1989 HMSO.

Horton, A. (1990) *The incest perpetrator, a family member no one wants to treat*, Sage

La Fontaine, J. (1990) *Child Sexual Abuse* Polity Press.

Lyon, C. and de Cruz, P. (1990) *Child Abuse* ,Family Law

Masson, J (1990) *The Children Act 1989 text and commentary*, Sweet and Maxwell

Morgan, J and Zedner, L (1992) *Child Victims*, OUP

Murray, K. and Gough, D. (1991) Implications and prospects in Murray, K. and Gough, D. (ed.) *Intervening in Child Sexual Abuse*, Scottish Academic Press.

Richardson, S. and Bacon, H. (1991) *Child Sexual Abuse: Whose Problem?* Venture.

Spencer, J. (1987) Child witnesses, Video technology and the law of evidence (1987) *Crim. Law Review*, 76.

Spencer, J. and Flin, R. (1990) *The evidence of children*, Blackstone Press.

Thoburn, J. (1991) The Children Act 1989. Balancing Child Welfare with the concept of partnership with parents, *J. Social Welfare and Family Law* (1991) 331-344.

Thoburn, J. (1992) Working Together and parental attendance at child care conferences 4 *Journal of Child Law*.

Viinikka, S. (1989) Child sexual abuse and the law in Driver, E. and Droisen, A. *Child Sexual Abuse: Feminist perspectives*, Macmillan.

Wattam, C. (1992) *Making a case in child protection*, Longmans.

3

Anti-racist child protection

Adèle Jones

Sivanandan, in his article 'Left, Right and Burnage' (1988) argues that there is no such thing as anti-racist ideology. He explores how the growing body of liberal thought and ideas umbrella'd within the term 'anti-racism' has reconstituted the fight against racism into a plea for multi-culturalism and 'positive action for ethnic minorities'. I shall, quite possibly, quite probably, explode the next time somebody refers to me as an 'ethnic minority'. Throughout my life as a Black woman, I have been defined and redefined by others — 'coloured', 'half-caste', mixed-race, mixed parentage and .....ethnic minority. It is as if my ethnicity (whatever that is) were the problem, as if the issue were to do with numbers or being in a minority, rather than to do with power and oppression. As if the lack of value and respect for cultural difference were the cause and not merely a symptom of racism. This is a distortion of the experience of Black people and a gross distortion of my concern for social equality. In so distorting the issues, the political energy and fire are taken out of the fight against racism, even as racism flourishes. As Sivanandan reminds us, it was racism that killed Ahmed Ullah back in 1986 at Burnage High School and anti-racism did not prevent his death. If there is no such thing as anti-racist ideology, then there can be no experts in anti-racist ideology. This is an important point, since it concerns the income of the increasing number of 'experts', Black and yes, white too, that have been spawned by the race relations industry and the market philosophy of this conservative era. Meanwhile racism, unabated by strategies on positive action, continues to cause the death of some children, like Ahmed, and harm to thousands of others. It is not that Sivanandan considers anti-racism unimportant. His argument is that there is 'no body of thought called anti-racism, no orthodoxy, or dogma, no manual of strategy and tactics, no demonology. If however, by anti-racism we mean 'against' racism then this has real value only if it is rooted in the fight against racism. This struggle is not lodged in a need for greater cultural understanding and tolerance, neither is it to be found in strategies for 'positive action for ethnic minorities'. It is part and parcel of the resistance to exploitation and an understanding of the nature of racism, its dehumanising and oppressive effects. It is from this perspective that I approach the subject of anti-racist child protection and readers who expect to find handy hints on working in a 'culturally sensitive' way should read no further; they will be disappointed.

So what then, is anti-racist child protection? Well firstly, in placing Black centre-stage, and not as a back-drop for white, we can see clearly that the current social work construction of child protection is yet another process through which racism is manifest. At a very simple level, any definition of child protection which does not address the protection of Black children from the harmful effects of racism and racial attacks must be challenged. Ensuring that all children have the right to protection from all forms of abusive power is central to anti-racist child protection work. However, this does not define it. There is no 'it' to define. What there is, as Bel Hooks [Race and Representation] points out, is our responsibility to critically evaluate and intervene in the system of which we have become a part. What there is, is a collection of thoughts and means, different and forever changing, used to combat the pervasive but also constantly changing, racist abuse of power. What I share then, are some of my thoughts about dealing with racism in child protection work. You must look for the means.

The themes that I wish to explore are:

- Current Social Work practice and procedures
- Perceptions of abuse.

Social Work Practice and Procedures

Child protection is the term used to cover the range of duties, responsibilities and powers that social workers and other professionals have in order to protect children from abuse and to prevent them from being harmed. It has become an area of work bound at one end by legal mandate and at the other by procedures and regulations, so much so that a professional vacuum has been created.

This makes it virtually impossible for parents, families and even those who have been abused, to assert that they have any expertise at all in the protection of children. The principle of 'partnership', one of the social work words for this decade, is, quite amazingly, applied to describe relationships with families who say they are willing to co-operate and accept decisions made. In a recent study I carried out for NSPCC in the North West, parents described feeling powerless and inadequate, their role in protecting their children being relegated to accepting the view the agency had of them and the decisions made. Anger and resistance, and even disagreement, understandable though these responses might be, were pathologised and used to reinforce the position and views of the agency. What is certain is that all children have the unequivocal right to protection from harm and abuse. What is less clear however, is how an approach that leaves parents feeling so powerless can at the same time 'empower' them (another 90's word) to fulfil their responsibilities to their children. While children are abused within their families, paradoxically it is also families, in the widest sense, that can provide the greatest protection from abuse.

If the 'professionalisation' of child protection has created a vacuum that prevents the full participation of parents and families, it has also provided a cover for institutionalising racism into the process. The guidance issued by the DoH (1988), described to me by a worker as the 'bible' for assessment work, provides an example of how any approach which fails to deal with inequality will itself become a tool for perpetuating it. It suggests that there are a number of factors which are significant in assessing parental background. Included among these factors are such things as poverty, persistent truanting/under-achievement at school and poor employment record/frequent moves/unemployed. Set within the context of indicators for child abuse, these factors are seen as the failings of individuals rather than as the product of social inequality.

The focus for intervention, concerned more with the failing individual than their social circumstances, masks the fact that poverty does indeed affect the ability of families to protect children. 'Under-achieving at school' and 'unemployed' are terms that are applied to Black people with a disproportionate frequency. This reflects different manifestations of racism. Any assessment process that sees these as the failings of Black people as indicators of child abuse rather than the effects of racial inequality, is in itself racist. One of the themes that all current social work legislation has in common is the emphasis on parental and family responsibility. This, ironically, runs hand in hand with a decrease in the resources that help families to fulfil their responsibilities. Decent housing and well-paid jobs contribute to the care and protection of children. While I am firmly opposed to the approach that suggests the absence of these leads inevitably mean higher risk for children, it is clear that such families are faced with a double-edged sword. On the one hand, these factors may be used to assess risk to children and on the other, little will be done to reduce these factors should they affect the family's ability to provide care for the child. In the case of the death of Tyra Henry, poverty and poor housing were key factors in Beatrice Henry's inability to protect her.

> There is an ever-present danger in social work .... of believing that the poor are so accustomed to poverty that they can be expected to get by in conditions which no middle class family would be expected to tolerate [London Borough of Lambeth, 1987].

Protecting Children, the Department of Health's (1988) guide on assessment, is incorrectly entitled. Guides and procedures such as this, whatever the intentions and however useful parts of them might be, lead us further and further into an approach that is more about protecting social work systems than it is about protecting children.

I am greatly concerned about the extent and effects of violence and oppression of children, not just nationally but globally. However, I fail to see how procedures, which often become ends in themselves, provide the resources to prevent child abuse. Although community care is considered as the poor relation of child protection social work, you can see parallels which perhaps make the point more clearly. Under the community care changes, my mother, who is disabled, is entitled to an assessment. She can even find out what the assessment criteria are and if she disagrees with the assessment she can use the complaints procedure. She may even have a care package put together for her and be appointed a care manager. All of these terms describe procedures and systems which require complex monitoring and regulation. My mother has no interest in them whatsoever; her concern is with the fact that because of the cuts in services she has to forego her daily bath.

The consequences of child protection work that focuses more on procedures than services are, of course, more serious. Children at risk of abuse in families are also exposed to it through social work. Many social workers have come to believe that the term 'child protection' justifies their intervention, whatever form that intervention takes. It does not. There are many people who have found the effects of social work intervention to be as great, and sometimes greater than the effects of abuse.

'I asked you to put an end to the abuse — you put an end to my whole family, you took away my nights of hell and gave me days of hell instead. You've exchanged my private nightmare for a very public one.' This is an indictment of social work and there is now a considerable body of evidence to show that not only is state intervention and care no guarantee of protection of children, it can also be harmful.

With regard to Black children, the prevalence of sexual and physical abuse is no different to that of white children. However, given that Black people are subjected to greater levels of poverty, unemployment and poor housing and given the use of these factors as indicators in assessment of potential child abuse, it is not unreasonable to suppose that Black people are facing higher levels of risk from the harmful effects of social work mis-intervention and misjudgement.

The social work of these times, particularly in relation to child protection, has become burdensome. In its attempts to become more effective, it has often, in reality become yet another millstone around the necks of children.

Any critic of the system is seen to condone liberal non-intervention and leaving children at risk. White workers, in their eagerness to throw off any charges of racism sometimes abdicate responsibility altogether and back off completely. Their passive 'right-on' poses are sometimes more dangerous than mis-intervention. Social work posturing and re-posturing on the topic leaves people confused and yet the myth that social workers are the experts is somehow maintained despite this. Even when the inadequacies and abuses of the system are exposed, through examples such as the gross abuse over many years of children in residential care in Leicestershire by Beck and the experiences of families in Cleveland, the impact is marginal. They are significant in the 'scandal' they cause, to use a media term, rather than the influence they have in challenging the current social work system.

The 1989 Children Act, noble though its principles might be, is collusive in the support of a system that requires fundamental change. Social work has taken on a deceit that is in keeping with an era of 'conservative cons' so that words like 'choice' and 'citizens' rights' disguise policies which result in an infringement of basic human rights and, through poverty and discrimination, the restriction of people's choices. Social work clients are now 'empowered'; they are ensured 'participation' and social workers will work in 'partnership' with them. These terms mask the fact that it is the disempowering effects of social work that need to be challenged and that allowing people to be partners in the care of their children is an indication of inequality rather than an attempt to redress it. The commitment to empowerment is both fragile and transparent — we have done nothing more than to intellectualise the term and build it in to our professional jargon.

The concerns about system abuse relate to all children, but given the impact of racism, Black children are disproportionately affected. As Bandana Ahmed points out: 'nowhere is abuse and oppression more exposed than through the Black experience'. Social work can only become an effective protector of children when it is prepared to tackle social inequality and injustice. While we need to develop more progressive ways of working with children and families, it is within this context that such developments should take place.

One particular example of progressive work that is worth exploring is the whanau decision making process that is used in New Zealand to protect and care for children. It is progressive not because it is new — in fact, it is based on Maori traditions that span centuries — but because it is set within the context of addressing social inequality and the racist outcomes of social work practice with indigenous Maori peoples.

The process is based on the belief that each family (that is, family in its widest sense) is the 'expert' on itself. It best knows its strengths, its problems and is best placed to determine what resources it needs in order to care for and support its members. It is in the family that decisions concerning the family should be made; it is here that the most appropriate decisions are made and where, when families make their own decisions, there is a commitment to make them work. In the field of child protection, workers have come to realise that while most abuse is caused by family members on their own children, the family can also provide better protection for children than the state. Families have the power and responsibility to make decisions about protecting children who have been harmed or are at risk and the professionals are invited to participate to provide information, support and resources.

The practice has developed out of the coming together of different struggles against racism and responds to the challenge issued by Te Kakapaiwaho Tibble: 'Return the authority of the tribes to the tribes, of the sub-tribes to the sub-tribes, of the families to the families, of the individuals to the individuals, who represent the multiple self of the generations of the past and the present' (Maori Economic Development Summit -Conference 1984).

It is important to note that the power for decision making is in the hands of the wider family and not just the nuclear family. The task of the social work agencies is to bring the family together irrespective of geographical and emotional boundaries in the interests of the child. Where parents object to the inclusion of the wider family, they may still be brought together based on the principle that the child has a right as an individual to the support and protection of wider family members, particularly, where risk to them might mean that they cannot continue living with their parents. The process is described fully in the publication *Family Decision Making*, Practitioner's Publishing, New Zealand 1991. These comments of workers, extracted from the publication, challenge many of the assumptions that currently hamper child protection work in this country.

'We have come to understand that:

- The people who get most deeply impassioned about a particular case of child abuse are the blood relatives.
- The people who have the most investment in protecting the child are the blood relatives.
- The people who understand the family dynamics best are blood relatives.
- Families hold information that workers can never access.

The myth of a child's safety in state care was exploded by the Department of Social Welfare Research which highlighted the level of sexual abuse of children while in the care of the state.

- Our acknowledgement of this stopped us demanding of families absolute guarantees of children's safety.
- Our acknowledgement of this helped us relinquish our investment in the old system.

The successful early outcomes of family decision making reinforced our commitment to this way of working.

- The families came up with a variety of alternatives greater than anything we could imagine or offer.

- The families took the responsibility for the children from us and if a decision did not work the family took the responsibility for making another decision.

- The families are the best source of information on which decisions can be made. We realised how inadequate our own assessments had been.'
  (*Family Decision Making*, 1991)

Perceptions of Abuse

Most attempts to define abuse fail to acknowledge the impact that racial abuse has on Black children. This omission at the very least denies the reality of the Black experience in Britain and also gives sanction to racism. Like other forms of abuse, racial abuse occurs in many ways including racial harassment, attacks and even death. A 1985 Home Office study revealed that there were 70,000 racial attacks each year. While these are not always targeted at children, being young is no protection and often whole families are attacked with no regard for the age or vulnerability of family members.

Violence perpetrated by those with racialist views is generally regarded as nothing to do with social work. Viewed as the extreme behaviour of a far-right minority, racial violence is not considered a significant enough issue to merit even a mention in child protection work. However, 70,000 attacks is hardly an insignificant number and in the cases of the eight Black people who lost their lives in racist murders in 1992, none of their murderers was a member of a far-right organisation. Far from being a 'minority' problem, racial violence is a feature of a society which creates the social conditions in which Black people are discriminated against.

Furthermore, by its failure to address racial violence, social work is sanctioning it. If as a social worker, your understanding of child physical and sexual abuse incorporates a feminist perspective which explores the ways in which violence and abuse of power are part of the process of socialisation, then you should understand that racial violence is a feature of and not separate from, the racism of society. Furthermore, if you subscribe to the view that pornography contributes to the development of an environment in which sexual

Fingerprints

I can see your fingerprints
fumbled all over this dead boy's body,
can see them in his
lifeless eyes,
in his fist clutched
by rigor mortis,
and holding up your hands to calm us people
you say: 'This was not a racial attack.'

I can see the wipe marks
on his forehead
where with the side of your fist
you tried to wipe them in
reshape them
rub them in
distort them
change them
hide them
rearrange them
with ink that dried
before he died
You report
'We understand the victim was Black.
This was not a racial attack.'

Lemn Sissay

abuse is deconstructed and rendered acceptable, then you should understand that racism is rendered acceptable by the state, its institutions, its legislation, the media etc.

An example of media distortion can be found in the coverage of the practice of placing Black children in Black foster homes. Violence between Black people in South Africa is termed 'Black on Black' violence; this contributes to a view that Black people are aggressive and uncivilised. However, the war in Bosnia, no less horrendous, is not termed 'white on white'. Similarly, the placement of Black children gets a very different treatment by the media than the placement of white children and similarly pervasively distorts truth. 'Same-race placement policies', 'political dogma of the extreme left' and even 'apartheid' are all terms used to describe practice for which

33

there is sound rationale. White children have always been cared for by white families, without media histrionics or 'extremist' labelling. The rationale for placing Black children in Black families lies within the struggle against racism and in the experiences of groups such as the Black and In Care National Steering Group. It is a feature of racism itself that such a rationale is necessary — there have been no equivalent debates about the placement of white children and it is ironic that when Black adults have sought to protect and support Black children, they themselves have been labelled as racist!

The CCETSW (1992) manual *Improving Practice with Children and Families* devotes a chapter to this topic and, in an exercise exploring media constructions, it asks the questions:

1. Why has the mainstream (white) media suddenly developed a concern for the fate of Black children? How does this concern with Black children who are in, or could be in, white families contrast with their lack of general concern about Black children? Coverage of the Deptford Fire in which thirteen Black children perished offers a salutary contrast here.

2. Why is all of the emphasis on the 'bannning' of white parents as substitute carers for Black children? What about the decades of policies and practices which have effectively 'banned' Black people as substitute carers?

3. Why is Black and anti-racist opposition labelled as 'politically motivated'? Why is a picture presented of the struggles of individuals against the might of the 'loony left', anti-racist bureaucracies? How is it that the notion of 'racism' is precisely turned on its head, that the realities of racism faced by Black people are denied and that when Black people dare to object to placement of Black children in white families, they are deemed 'racist'?

4. Who does the white media turn to for testimony? Who are the experts? Whose stories are heard? Why is the hurt suffered by white people seen as the most important? (CCETSW Curriculum Development Project Publication Two).

The placement of Black children in Black families is about the protection of those children. It is a child protection issue. Undue focus on the issue tends to distract from other issues such as the high numbers of Black children in local authority care and their vulnerability to poverty and poor housing. These factors are part of the wider context of racism which affect the life chances of Black children in fundamental ways. It will affect where they live, their income, where or if they work, their education, their health, their safety and their relationships with others. Contrary to popular media interpretation, Black children are not helped to deal with the effects of this type of abuse by being rescued by white people. Not only will they still be exposed to racism, they will be less equipped to challenge and deal with it. There are Black people who have grown up in care who claim not to have experienced racism, as if the greater identification and familiarity with white folks reduces the likelihood! Unfortunately, the manifestations of racism are not within the control of individuals or groups who are its victims and racism is not destroyed by a failure to acknowledge it. If anything is reduced, it is the ability to challenge it.

A further problem for Black children growing up apart from Black adults is the reconstruction by white and Black people of identity. We have moved out of the period in which difference was played down and integration into a norm that valued only white, English orthodoxy was the bench-mark of having cared well for Black children. Now, in the concern not be seen to devalue Black children (while continuing to devalue their Black parents), cultural heritage is defined and objectified into static ethnic packaging. Parts of being Black are turned into commodities, while other parts are rejected. Black identity is reconstructed and sold back to us. We are told that to be Black you have to fit into the slot you have been allotted. For Black children growing up in care without the diversity, the richness, the collective wisdoms and foolishnesses, without the strengths and strategies of Black peoples, there is a danger that they come to fit the slot and lose themselves or deny themselves altogether.

A young person from the Manchester Black and In Care Group describes the way in which she was affected by this process. 'The image of myself was reflected back as an image associated with drugs, violence, simpleness, exotic, problematic, bad, mad. From the time I first saw and heard, all the positive images I was provided with were of white people and I did not exist as myself or only in someone else's design.' Black people have long since understood that minimising the effects of this form of abuse means providing children with care that builds self-esteem, strengths and strategies for dealing with racism. It is this knowledge that lies behind the struggle of the last decade for the right of Black children not to be removed from their families in the first case and, when it is inevitable, for them to be cared for by Black adults.

As with other forms of abuse, it is the survivors who highlight best the struggles and strategies that helped them to deal with the personal effects of abuse.

Anti-racist child protection is concerned not only with challenging the racism in child protection procedures and within society generally, it is also concerned with the violence that Black children experience within their families. This is not different from the violence that white children experience within their families and nor is it separate from the violence children are subjected to globally.

Gifts From My Grandmother

A long overdue poem to my eyes
Poor brown slit eyes
You cause me so much pain
But for you, I would be
Totally invisible.
When young
You filled with tears
At the slightest provocation
When children teased
It was because of you
They hated me.
In story books,
Her big blue eyes opened wide
But you, you narrowed into slits.

Hard brown slit eyes
Echoes of the pain
You mirror back the world,
And I can see them all,
Drowning there..

Soft brown slit eyes
Windows of the soul
I can see you staring back
Frank, open, lovely.

Meiling Jin

Furthermore, violence imposed upon children and violence imposed upon women are inextricably connected. These issues have not been covered here; they are another chapter in the book.

References:

CCETSW (1992) *Anti-Racist Social Work Education 'Improving Practice with Children and Families'* London: CCETSW

Department of Health (1988) *Protecting Children: a guide to social workers undertaking a comprehensive assessment* London: HMSO

'Fingerprints' by Lemn Sissay is taken from *The Sun Rises in the North*, Smith/Doorstep Books

Hooks, Bel (1992) *Black Looks : race and representation*, London, Turnaround

Jones, Adèle (1991) *Black and In Care* (Report to NSPCC 'Saying It As It Is') London: NSPCC

Maori Economic Development Summit Conference (1984) *Tibble Paper No 58* Maori Conference Proceedings, New Zealand

Meiling, Jin (1991) *Gifts From My Grandmother* New Zealand, Practitioners' Publishing

Practitioners' Publishing (1991) *Family Decision Making.*

Sivanandan, A. (1988) 'Left, Right and Burnage' *New Statesman*, 27.5.88

4

Multiprofessionalism and the Children Act 1989: a paediatrician's view

Nick Spencer

Introduction

The 1989 Children Act has been described as the most comprehensive and far-reaching reform of child law in living memory. The Act
affects all aspects of child care work and is appropriate and timely
for multidisciplinary perspectives on the Act and its implications to
be shared.

I am a community paediatrician; the focus of my work is the
primary and secondary prevention of childhood ill-health and the
protection of children from abuse in all its forms, societal as well as
intrafamilial. In European terms I would be described as a social
paediatrician in that I am concerned with the effects of social and
environmental factors on child health. Prior to taking up my present
post, I worked for ten years as a paediatrician straddling the hospi-
tal/community divide in a post created in response to the Court
Report (HMSO, 1976); child protection work, both clinical and multi-
professional, formed an important element of my work.

Before moving to the main body of my contribution, it is worth
describing very briefly the Chair of Community Paediatrics at Warwick, as it is a unique example, in the UK at least, of a multiprofessional approach to child care. The Chair is in two university
departments; the School of Postgraduate Medical Education and the
Department of Applied Social Studies, which is, amongst other
things, a social work training and research department. Thus, the
multiprofessional model is brought together in one appointment.
The marriage, like most, is not always happy and entails many

difficult compromises but the prospects for conceiving mould-breaking and innovative off-spring, both in joint teaching initiatives and research, are considerable. As I will argue later, multiprofessional training and research are essential components in the development of genuine 'working together'.

In this paper, I will consider some general issues raised by the 1989 Children Act and multiprofessional working from a paediatric perspective, before moving on to specific issues for child health workers and some thoughts on future developments and the potential paediatric contribution to 'working together' in the new climate created by the Children Act.

Some general issues

One of the key underlying principles of the Act is the 'paramountcy principle' whereby the welfare and interests of the children are seen to be paramount. This is a welcome recognition of the need for legal and professional agencies to 'put the child first'; however, paramountcy carries with it some important and difficult dilemmas.

Despite major demographic change, most children continue to live in families with at least one consistent adult carer, usually the child's mother. Decisions related to the child's best interests are frequently complicated by the close bonds which have been established between children and their main carers, and in situations of suspected abuse, the apparent advantages of separation must be weighed against the dangers inherent in breaking or weakening those bonds. Health professionals are frequently able to identify the potential for harm from continued parental responsibility resting with main carers; however, we frequently avoid the equally important issue of the potentially harmful effect of separation. The Act attempts to address this issue through the 'no-order' principle.

Similarly, because the child's experiences has been confined to a specific family setting, the welfare of the child is difficult to define as an entity separate from that of the family. Undoubtedly, there are situations where it is beyond dispute that the welfare of the child is best protected outside the family but in many cases no such certainty exists and the 'paramountcy principle' is difficult to apply.

A major advance represented by the Act is the recognition that the child's own views are important in relation to their welfare. The need to seek the child's views when appropriate is one means by which the dilemmas posed by separation can be addressed, though not always resolved. For too long professionals have assumed they knew what was 'in the child's best interests'. Such assumptions are no longer acceptable; our practice must change to accommodate the child's own view.

Here also the issues are by no means straightforward. We have little or no experience of genuinely consulting children on their wishes and children themselves may be placed in the impossible position of choosing between 'the devil and the deep blue sea'. We all need help, guidance and training in the new discipline of listening and responding appropriately to the child's view.

An equally important shift of emphasis represented by the Act is the recognition of parental responsibility and parental involvement in decision-making related to their children. Like the child as active participant, effective and genuine parental participation poses many problems for professionals accustomed to reaching decisions in multiprofessional groups from which parents are excluded. Within child health care, considerable experience has been gained in recent years in the development of partnership with parents, notably in the care of children with handicapping conditions (Brimblecombe and Russell, 1988) and the lesson of this work can inform and guide the process of involving parents in a genuine partnership to protect their children.

The 'paramountcy principle' and the active involvement of children and parents in decision-making focus on the child in the family and on child protection as a primarily intra-familial issue. Most professional practice has this focus and it is consistent with the predominant philosophy of individual responsibility. The Act's concern with 'children in need' and the placing of responsibility with Local Authorities for identifying and providing services for these children tends to shift the focus from individual to societal responsibility for child care. This is to be welcomed though the major funding implications of the shift have not been adequately addressed.

The Act's definition of 'children in need', covering as it does children unlikely to achieve or maintain a reasonable standard of health or development, children whose health and development is likely to be significantly impaired and children with disabilities, should encompass children suffering the effects of poverty (Lowe, 1991) as well as those suffering specific illnesses and developmental delay. If resources were made available for provision of the recommended services for all these children this would represent a major change. However, it is clear that the responsibility for the operational definition, and the consequent funding, is being pushed onto local government (Carlton, 1991) without a unifying central approach to definition and without additional funds from central government.

The provision of services to 'children in need' is seen in the Act as a necessary part of child protection and the prevention of future harm to children. Social, education and health services are charged with the task of identifying 'children in need' and ensuring their needs are met. This would seem to be a golden opportunity for local agencies to develop a common strategy for child protection which goes beyond procedures for responding to suspected intra-familial abuse and builds on untapped community resources and experience from community-based projects in the US and elsewhere (Chamberlin, 1987).

Specific issues for paediatricians and child health workers

Child health workers, and particularly paediatricians, have tended to adopt an approach to child protection work based on the assumption that medical expertise is the most important and the paediatrician's assessment should be given priority. Other professional groups have colluded in this process which, in some cases, has rendered multiprofessional working impossible. Equally, doctors have resisted sharing information with clients and have favoured a paternalistic communication style.

Thus, the changes required by the Children Act pose some particular problems for paediatricians. Not least among these is the participation of parents in the decision-making process related to their children and the requirement to make clinical information and judgements available to parents.

Parental participation

The Act seeks to foster partnership between professionals and parents in the protection of children. Paediatricians have moved some way towards partnership in other areas of child health work (see above) but the forfeit of power implied in genuine partnership does not come easily to a profession used to a position of power and autonomy in decision-making and treatment. In the area of child protection the power relationships are necessarily more one-sided (Tunnard & Ryan, 1991); however, parental involvement in the decision-making process and the availability of the right to see records, to appeal and to complain should provide some balance without jeopardising the child's safety. Indeed there is some evidence (see Thoburn, 1992) that parental involvement in case conferences strengthens rather than weakens the individual child protection plan.

Participation of the child

Equally threatening to the paternalistic approach is the need to consult the child and seek their consent to examination. As paediatricians, we have assumed that we communicate well with children and listen to their viewpoint. In child protection, the reality, however, has been different; all too frequently 'things have been done to children' without their consent and with little or no explanation (Cleveland Inquiry, HMSO, 1988). Our practice must change to give the child an element of control. The consent of children of 'sufficient maturity' should be sought for any medical examinations or procedures and careful explanations, appropriate to the child's development level, should be given to all children, young as well as old, prior to examination.

'Sufficient maturity' is ill-defined in the Act. Some countries such as the Netherlands have opted for a specified age limit (above 9 years); however, I feel that the lack of precision in the Act is a potential advantage as chronological age is a poor indicator of maturity. Professionals working together with the Courts will have to establish working definitions of 'sufficient maturity' and health professionals will have the lead role in applying these in individual cases. Undoubtedly, dilemmas will arise when children refuse consent for a crucial examination or opt for a course of action which the professional agencies find dangerous; however, the opportunity for children to participate in decisions affecting their lives is a positive step in line with the UN Convention on the Rights of the Child (1989) and professional agencies must work together to ensure that the child's rights are not lost in the rush to 'protect the child'.

'Children in need'

Many children with disabilities are seen regularly by paediatric services as well as children with other chronic conditions which fall within the Act's definition of 'children in need'. In addition, children and families in poverty are heavy users of the paediatric services. Paediatricians have the potential to play a key role in the identification of 'children in need' as well as to influence local government decisions related to the breadth of the definition applied. I say 'potential' deliberately, as many paediatricians continue to regard their main function as the treatment of the disease process in the individual child, without reference to social and environmental influences which act both to precipitate the disease and to perpetuate its effects. The development of community-based paediatrics with its orientation to 'population paediatrics' and the management of children outside the hospital setting is encouraging a shift in attitudes and the Paediatrician as Child Advocate is increasingly gaining acceptance (Macfarlane, 1993).

Special needs registers have been developed by paediatric services in some areas and by Education Departments; under the requirements of the Act these will have to be extended to include other 'children in need' or separate registers established for different groups of children. It seems logical to combine the registers using a common data base in collaboration with Social Service and Education Departments. Registration criteria will depend on the breadth of the definition of 'children in need' and should reflect a consensus across the agencies. Registers are difficult to maintain. Community-based paediatric services could take lead responsibility with funding assistance from the other interested agencies.

Parental suspicion of registers should be acknowledged and the data on individual children only entered with informed parental, and, when appropriate, child consent. Parental fears will be allayed only when registers for 'children in need' are shown to benefit the children and families themselves. Parents should be consulted on a regular basis to ensure that the information is accurate and up-to-date and to involve parents in determining the most appropriate uses of the data.

Minimising delay

Delay in deciding a child's future is particularly damaging and the Act requires decisions to be taken with the minimum delay. Medical reports are often crucial evidence and the paediatrician's opinion may be essential to the Court's decision. Equally, the new orders under the Act are strictly time-limited, making the often leisurely pace of past investigations untenable. Along with other agencies, paediatric practice will need to change to accommodate the new time limits and ensure early decision-making.

Some thoughts on future working

The theme of these papers is multiprofessional working. The Children Act as a whole obliges agencies to concentrate on the welfare and well-being of the child and to break down barriers based on inter-agency suspicion. Multiprofessional working should not involve the formation of an elite circle of child protection workers which excludes colleagues and families; it should form the basis of an open approach to the difficult and challenging problems of child welfare and protection. Particular attention should be paid to refining techniques for joint working and information recording and ensuring active parental and child participation in decision-making.

The challenge to provide for 'children in need' raises the key issue of community-wide strategies for child welfare and protection. The development of such strategies, involving professionals, voluntary agencies and local communities, shifts the emphasis of child protection work from the individual family to the societal and environmental influences on child welfare. It also raises uncomfortable issues related to the increase in child poverty and its implications for child protection. Provision for 'children in need' includes advocacy on behalf of children and pressure on government, local and national, to adopt social policies which strengthen rather than weaken family functioning. All too often, in recent years, parents have been blamed and castigated for failing to care adequately for their children whilst social policy decisions have been made which force families further into debt and increase family poverty.

A further key area for development is talking to children and representing their views. We are inexperienced in this area and much work needs to be done. Small groups of professionals have become expert in this area but, if we are to carry out the requirements of the Act, these skills need to be more widely available. There are major training implications; not all professionals will want or be able to undertake this work but, in each area, special provision should be made for training those with an aptitude and an interest. All professionals working with children should be aware, at the very least, of the importance of the child's view even if they are not skilled enough to ascertain it.

A final thought is that many of the provisions of the Children Act seem to me to support the establishment of a system of Family Courts based on a non-adversarial approach to child care. These are well-established in other European countries and experience suggests that the form encourages family and child participation.

In conclusion, the Children Act is a major and important piece of legislation with implications for all those working with children. The Act has been broadly welcomed by paediatricians; however, as I have indicated, it challenges many of our practices and forces us to think beyond the narrow confines of the 'medical model'.

References

Brimblecombe, F. and Russell, P. (1988) *Honeylands: developing a service for families with handicapped children* London. National Children's Bureau.

Carlton, J. (1991) The Children Act and Social Services. *Children and Society*, Vol. 5:4;21-27.

Chamberlin, R. (ed) (1988) *Beyond individual risk assessment: community wide approaches to promoting the health and development of families and children.* Washington, USA. The National Center for Education in Maternal and Child Health.

HMSO (1976) *Fit for the Future (The Court Report): the Report of the Committee on Child Health Services* London, HMSO.

HMSO (1988) *Report of the Inquiry into Child Abuse in Cleveland 1987.* London, HMSO.

Lowe, R. (1991) The Children Act and Health Professionals. *Children and Society*, Vol.5:4;52-57.

Macfarlane, J.A. (1993) Health Promotion and children and teenagers. Editorial, *British Medical Journal*, January 9th, 306;81.

Thoburn, J. (ed) (1992) *Participation in Practice — involving families in Child Protection: a reader.* Norwich. Social Work Development Unit, University of East Anglia.

Tunnard, J. and Ryan, M. (1991) What does the Children Act mean for Family Members? *Children and Society*, Vol.5:4;67-75.

United Nations Convention on the Rights of the Child, adopted by the UN General Assembly, November 1989; ratified by the British Government December, 1991.

5

Child-centred Teamwork in Practice

Margaret Randall and Su Beech

The following is an account of one project's struggle to offer child-centred, therapeutic services to its local community. In thinking about 'child-centred' work practice, we needed to consider both the child's outer world and inner world experiences and our own within-project teamwork (how we functioned as a team) and outer teamwork (our relationship with the child's entire network) — a process that came to be known as 'safety networking'.

The project, the Elms Project, is an NSPCC initiative, delivering services to the Borough of Sandwell. Its remit was to set up psychotherapeutic services to children, young people and their families and carers, who have either experienced abuse (sexual, emotional and physical) or who are at risk of significant harm. This latter 'at risk of significant harm' category was agreed to include children and young people who posed a risk to themselves, who might be in danger of harming themselves, such as a suicidal child or adolescent, a child with an uncontrolled physical disorder, for example diabetes, or a child with autism. In practice, services have been provided to the many children and young people who have experienced sexual abuse and/or physical abuse and/or emotional abuse.

All project members are funded by the NSPCC, either as full-time employees or on a freelance basis and are involved in some capacity with BTPP, the Birmingham based training school for child psychoanalytic psychotherapy.

One year on, the project is staffed by an Area Children's Services Manager (a Social Worker and trainee Child Psychotherapist), a Project Leader (a Social Worker and trainee Child Psychotherapist), a Social Worker (and future trainee child psychotherapist), two

47

further trainee Child Psychotherapists, (one a former Social Services Team leader who will move on to the developing NSPCC Shropshire base, and the second a Chartered Clinical Psychologist), the part-time Regional Consultant to the NSPCC — a Principal Child Psychotherapist, and the Organising Tutor for BTPP; a Project Administrator and a Project Secretary.

In its early stages the Elms Project was developed as a multi-disciplinary project to include Local Authority sponsored workers from psychiatry, clinical psychology, health visiting, and Social Services. For several reasons this did not work out in practice. There were difficulties with funding and a growing difficulty in work practice, based on trying to work together with others with different methods of working.

To describe the first few months of caseworking as 'stressful' would be an understatement. Not only were Child Psychotherapy services being introduced to the Borough's Child Protection services and vice versa, but a parallel process was occurring within the project team itself and within the NSPCC organisation as a whole. The Elms had been known as a Child and Family Centre and existing team members had been involved with disclosure work and other therapeutic approaches, often based on a family therapy or co-working model, with one person talking with the child or family, another taking notes and offering live supervision and perhaps another viewing from behind a one-way screen. This meant that within the team, let alone outside it, virtually all aspects of work practice had to be re-examined and debated. It was a painful and draining time for all. The psychotherapy team had to evolve — its membership, its work practices — at a time of major organisational change within the NSPCC.

The first case on which the project worked psychodynamically proved to be a test case, in many ways. It threw up a whole array of issues with which we had to grapple, within the team, within the NSPCC organisation and within the local authority network.

It arose from a written referral, received from a Local Authority Social Worker requesting, 'joint work by representatives of the two agencies'. It concerned a 5 year old boy, Robert, who had been accommodated by the local authority for the past 15 months. Robert was the eldest of four children, had been rejected by his parents and was to remain in care, with the possibility of being freed for adoption. He had unsupervised home weekend access with his two parents. Robert had recently disclosed being sexually abused by the twenty year old son of the first foster family with whom he had been placed. [He was now engaging in 'sexual antics' with his siblings and other children in the foster home, would wet himself frequently and masturbated regularly whatever the setting]. Robert had already received self-protection work, along the lines of naming body parts, appropriate and inappropriate touching and saying 'No'.

The case was discussed and it was agreed that two project members should meet with the Social Worker for a fact finding discussion.

The family history revealed two parents, one 16 and the other 18 years old at Robert's conception, and both with their own family histories of neglect, isolation, instability, violence and crime. We were told that his mother had never taken to Robert from birth and on first seeing him had thought 'what have I got this for?' Presumably father had not taken to him either. This was therefore a family in which, for literally generations no-one had experienced any good measure of parental containment.

When Robert was three years old, his young mother had become so depressed as to warrant psychiatric admission. This was to be Robert's first experience of care, for a period of one week. A year later she re-referred herself saying she was unable to cope with the children. Father had left the home, as he had on many previous occasions, when he felt the pressure of family life became too great. So Robert was placed with his second set of foster carers for three days, then with a third set, for a period of seven weeks. Unfortunately, these foster carers felt unsafe since they knew Robert's extended family and thought the situation could become violent. Robert went on to his fourth set for a month but, not surprisingly considering the disruption he was experiencing, these foster carers found him unmanageable so Robert was moved on to his fifth set where he settled, or rather where they hung onto him, for 15 months, the point at which the project became involved. Robert's three siblings had remained at home after Robert's second experience of care.

The age at which Robert was moved and the periods of time he stayed in each placement were finally pieced together. It was crucial information, that was not fully grasped until well into the work and the report writing. We wondered why this had happened and thought it had much to do with the enormity of its emotional impact. With many such cases concerning similar family backgrounds, children suffer the impact of multiple separations, so traumatic and damaging to such a very young child, repeatedly. It does sound awful to describe Robert's case and situation as typical but it was and still is. In reality, there are many children, entire families of children, who have had, to the outside world, far worse experiences than Robert. It can be tempting to describe these by no means unusual Social Services family histories in terms of 'oh you know, the usual — locked in their room, given mouldy food to eat, no lightbulbs.' Such flippancy is one way of trying to deal with the awfulness of such situations. We were to find that guiding the Social Worker through the emotional impact of the (exploratory) *process* that was to follow was to be one of our essential roles, one element of the safety networking.

In the course of our initial meeting, the Social Worker told us how Robert's mother had been repulsed by the sexual abuse and Robert's sexually explicit behaviour; how his father managed to attend medicals with him but was devastated and overwhelmed when he came upon Robert having what was called 'oral sex' with his younger sister. Robert had not been home since. Robert was now a chronic bed wetter. He would often run up to his foster mother and wet in front of her.

We concluded this preliminary meeting by agreeing to take the information back to the team for discussion and to get in touch again as soon as possible. This would give us essential time to stop and think how to approach the request and the case, and what plan to put on offer.

Shortly after this, the Social Worker made contact again to tell us that Robert's behaviour was deteriorating; he was a danger to other children at school, was on the verge of being excluded (we later found out Robert had already come close to being excluded from another primary school and his behaviour had been notably difficult in Nursery) and had been observed by his teacher engaging in dubious activities with a group of other boys, in the toy telephone box. They had scattered very rapidly when the teacher had gone across to investigate. What had actually been going on no-one could know for sure — Robert had gained a reputation and might have been suffering from this, but certainly people were very concerned for him and rattled by him. The teacher thought another worker, a psychologist, should become involved. This was a point at which we felt we were losing our grip and that there was a danger of professional 'overkill'; a number of people being brought in at the same time, falling over each other and creating further tangles in an already complex situation.

Meanwhile we were, as a team, discussing ways of working. In the past, it would not have been unusual to have taken on Robert for direct work, to have co-worked with the Social Worker — two workers together with the child. Sessions would have been partly prepared beforehand, with various exercises. The Social Worker would have then had direct access to the session contents.

From the initial discussion we felt Robert was a child about whom we should be very concerned and we decided it was essential for us to get to know more about him. There was a picture forming of a severely deprived child and possibly a severely disturbed one. His history was one of non-containment from birth. We suspected his wetting was a concrete and graphic sign of this; he could not hold anything in, either physically or emotionally, because he had never had the experience of being held psychologically. Also there seemed to be something about Robert that caused people to reach the ends of their tethers rather rapidly and then expel him. Did Robert project, that is put into others, some inner chaos with such force that he was experienced as intolerable and unholdable? We suspected this might be the case and, if so, was Robert heading for more moves, and with what end result? What would be the impact of this on his development, on his relationships, his ability to learn and keep himself (and others) safe?

Margaret Randall was assigned to the direct work with Robert, and Su Beech to the work with the foster carers, throughout the whole exploratory process. This support of parents/carers is as vital an element in the process as is seeing the child.

Our offer of a series of exploratory sessions to determine Robert's needs created much tension. It would involve Robert meeting with Margaret Randall for a series of 6 sessions — which, on reflection, was too many. Three would have been enough since Robert quickly formed an attachment, based on his considerable need — an attachment which could not be pursued. Telephone calls went to and fro between ourselves and the social worker. Why was real work, that is something more active or more directed towards the problems, not being done, when Robert's behaviour was deteriorating by the day? This was not a criticism; it was a genuine question. The Social Worker was receiving telephone calls himself from all quarters. Results were required, or rather hoped for — the urgency of Robert's needs being put into the work process (i.e. something had to be done now and quickly) rather than being seen, more painfully, as an indication of Robert's inner chaos and desperation. Taking a measured approach, doing an assessment, would necessarily mean that upset could and would be more in evidence with all its consequences to all parties involved.

Also, with hindsight it seems possible that the nature of these exploratory sessions needed more explanation than we realised at the time. We had in mind an assessment of Robert's present and future needs, based on his level of disturbance — particularly where he might live and the level of therapeutic input he would most likely need. By doing this we hoped to find a way forward for Robert by using the conclusions to inform the adults around him and make plans for him, solidly based on who he was.

The Social Worker did agree to the idea of the exploratory sessions but then the next hurdle came into sight. A workers' meeting was agreed as a next step but who should be invited to attend? The old team had two views, hinging around Robert's foster carers. One was that the foster carers were workers, fellow professionals, who had almost always, if not routinely, been involved in workers' meetings. But should foster carers be exposed to a lot of sorting out and setting up which had to be done between the 'professionals'? Did workers need a private space too, in which to thrash out ideas and say what they really meant, without fear of losing face or being criticised by others in front of people more intimately involved with their clients, such as foster carers? There were definite echoes of 'what about the workers'? Were foster carers foster carers or foster parents? Should people in actual parental roles (those who do the washing and ironing, cope with the outbursts of upset and temper) really be expected, in a burdensome way, to be members of the professional caring profession too? At no time was the foster carers' role seen as anything less than vital. But not to invite them was seen by some as a dismissing exclusion rather than as a protection based on valuing or as good boundary keeping.

With real misgivings, openly expressed, the social worker convened the meeting as we had asked. That is, Robert's foster carers were not invited but had been told that such a meeting was going ahead. They made no objection as such; they would have liked to have been there but seemed to be generally quite accepting. Robert's parents were informed too. The networks involved with Robert's case were typical of those involved in such cases. There was the Local Authority Social Worker, the Homefinding Link Worker, the Deputy Head of Robert's school, the Family Centre Worker (from the Centre where the self-protection work had been carried out) who worked one-to-one with both Robert's mother and father, Robert's foster carers and Robert's parents. Later an Educational Psychologist joined the network as did Robert's class teacher. There were four people from our team; the direct worker, the foster carers' worker, and two managers, one holding the Child Protection/NSPCC function and the other the Child Psychotherapy function. Members of this team had not worked together before.

The first workers' meeting was an uneasy one. It began by both the social workers and the Link Worker formally registering their concern that Robert's foster carers had not been invited to attend. The atmosphere was very tense. But a much fuller picture of Robert emerged. The Deputy Head had liaised closely with Robert's class teacher and told us how Robert directed his aggressive behaviours towards other boys — he would bite them, drag them about, poke them with his pencil, deliver head butts and flood the toilets. He was very reluctant to go out to play at break times and was generally highly disruptive. We heard how Robert could respond positively to his teacher when asked to do various errands but how this often changed, abruptly, into a disruptive incident and was in effect, spoilt or destroyed. Robert would totally deny his involvement in any incident, not just fibbing or being defiant displaying an alarming and real wiping out of awareness. Robert was no ordinary distressed child.

The meeting gelled as we all agreed Robert was in deep trouble and moved towards setting up the exploratory sessions. Questions were raised about how the information gained from each session would be relayed to, for example, the social worker and Robert's foster mother. Would they be given a brief outline at the end of each session? Discussions about a child's rights to confidentiality ensued. Were we being secretive, uncooperative, elitist? Finally the social worker and I agreed to differ, which, in retrospect was a great act of faith on his behalf. After all he would be the one on the front line explaining all this to Robert's parents. With the members of the meeting still present, the social worker phoned Robert's foster mother who immediately agreed to accompany Robert to and from his sessions (as we had hoped) and meet with Su Beech, first at home then at The Elms. It was agreed that both Su and the Link Worker would go along to the first meeting with the foster parents at their home. The social worker would have the considerable and complex responsibility of maintaining contact with Robert's parents, the foster carers, the school, the Educational Psychologist and with us.

This he did. With the exploratory process underway, it seemed the social worker would phone Su Beech one time and Margaret Randall another. This made us ensure that we had our act together, so that we could give consistent, thought-out responses to the difficult situations with which the social worker was having to deal. Robert's parents were asking for contact; the social worker was wondering about our views. Bearing in mind that Robert had not seen them for some time, we thought that if they could be dissuaded from doing so, at least until the exploratory sessions were complete, that would on balance be helpful to us and probably to Robert. He was bursting at his emotional seams as it was.

Robert's parents agreed to a postponement, with not a little relief. What parents, whatever their problems and past histories, would not wish to see their child when in the middle of a process which they knew could easily result in Robert living elsewhere on a long-term basis. Ambivalence is a part of life and present in all major decision-making processes. Robert's parents needed to be allowed to express their wish to have their son home for a visit, to see themselves as parents who cared, even though they also knew they did not have the capacity to really look after and care for him on an everyday basis. So when the social worker said, in effect, 'yes, I know you want him home for a while but I also know you know, with the best will in the world, you cannot care for him', their ambivalence was acknowledged. They were not pushed into an 'either/or' position so were able to think about their son in a most helpful and unselfish way.

The next stage was to see Robert and his foster parents. More preparation was required. In which room would Robert be seen at The Elms? What about an individual box of items for Robert and only Robert to use during the exploratory sessions; items which would help him express the thoughts and feelings which often cannot be put into words?

The only room available at the time was a rather large one, fitted with a one-way screen, complete with wall-mounted video camera and microphone. It had an alcove with shelving, pictures on the walls, attractive toys and games around the place; even a punch ball and a toy telephone box (which Robert would later put to good use) and a heavy ashtray. With the benefit of hard-earned past experience we tidied away as much as possible and removed the lower shelves so Robert would not be able to climb up them. This created some puzzlement among other people in the building. Might it be being rather unfriendly to have such a bare room? The room was L-shaped, so it was possible for someone to be just out of view, round the corner. We were glad when, soon after this piece of work, standard practices were enforced to make rooms safe — safety glass put into windows, fire extinguishers removed and general measures taken to make the environment as safe as possible for a child who might only be able to act our their pain by attacking themselves, the worker or the room.

There was also 'the box', so often mentioned by child psychotherapists, seen by some as a 'box of tricks', shrouded in mystery. But there was no mystery — it was a strong plastic box, containing stationery items, such as felt pens, pencil, sharpener, rubber and paper, and other toys like a family of dolls, a car, a police car and ambulance, plasticine and so on, à la Melanie Klein, one of the pioneers of child psychotherapy. What was going to be done with this box and with Robert? It was tempting to say 'nothing' — which is not as rude or misleading as it sounds. The idea was to introduce Robert to his worker and the session, then to his box and to see what happened next, in terms of what he did, how he did it, how he related to his worker and most importantly what it all felt like to the worker as it happened. His worker was not there to play with him or direct him (except when he was putting himself or the worker at risk of being hurt or when causing wanton damage to the room) but to notice and try to talk to him about what he was doing and what it might mean, what he might be trying to say, with and without words. There is no magic recipe for this procedure either — just a solid training and hard work on the part of the worker.

To give a flavour of the work, here are some extracts from detailed session notes, written up after each session and used for supervision purposes. All such notes are held for personal training purposes so are not held on file nor are they identifiable. For the purposes of this paper Robert's details have been disguised. Both he and his parents have moved out of the area.

To quote from the first session:

> They were 10 minutes late. Su and I met them in reception; Robert, his foster mother and another foster child, Lee aged 11 years. Foster mother was very apologetic — they had had difficulty in finding the building. I was unsure which child was Robert but guessed he must be the shorter of the two, being the younger at 5 years old. Foster mother said she must go and park the car properly.

I introduced myself to foster mother and Robert and suggested we go into the room in which we would be working, having pointed to the room across the corridor where his foster mother would be. Robert made a step forward, keeping his gaze on foster mother as she prepared to leave. He peered into the other room and said brightly 'there's turtles in that room.' He wasn't hallucinating, just referring to another child's painting of the Ninja Turtles pinned up on the wall. I suggested we go into our room and he looked up at Su enquiringly. He then turned and grinned up at me and went readily into the room.

He walked a few paces then stopped and stood still, looking around. He seemed small and a little lost. I said how it was a strange place for him which he had not been to before, and with me, someone he had not met before. He turned and grinned.

I pointed out the box to him, which sat on the coffee table in the middle of the room, just in front of him. I said that the things in it were for him to use during the times that we met, to help us to think about him and for him to tell or show me what he had to say. He immediately reached for the police car and held it out to me, smiling, saying 'Look!' He struck me as bright and alert but somehow unconnected or vaguely vacant. I realised I was sitting on the edge of my chair, with Robert kneeling at the table. I felt vulnerable to some attack from him, leaning forwards towards him as I was. He seemed interested in the tow bar, calling it by some name like 'thingy'. I also realised I had not talked about the structure of the session, the length of time or anything (which was, in part, to do with Robert's willingness to go off with a stranger — which is quite a common characteristic of children who have little sense of themselves, of being attached to others and feeling they belong). But I struggled to explain, sounding as though I did not know what I was talking about. Robert did not appear to hear a word and seemed 'shut off'.'

Then, to quote from the session some twenty minutes later:

He walked back to the table. The men figures fought, kicking each other in the face. He said the red one had won and he knocked over the others, one by one. He closely examined their faces. He said they were more angry. When I said I thought he was feeling like that too, he said he did — sometimes — then became excited in a frenetic way.

There were more voices off. He said 'Where's Lee and what's he doing?' and walked towards the door, about to leave the room. I said 'I'd like you to stay in the room so we can think about what's going on'. He stopped and looked at me in surprise then turned his attentions to 'Postman Pat' (one of the old NSPCC collecting boxes) in the corner to the right of the door. He ran his finger over the two slots, one in his cap and the other in the actual collecting box. He returned to the table and pointed up to the wall mounted microphone. I said it was a microphone and that it was not switched on. He went over to the telephone box, got inside and dialled and listened, looking back gleefully, listening to the voices. He again asked for money, as if he had no recollection of having already asked me. He said he needed 'something thin to fit in'. He came over to the box and looked inside and found the pencil sharpener, remarking on the 'big and little holes'. I said 'rather like us; one big one and one little one'. He smiled, with what I thought was understanding and put the pencil in the little hole, saying 'it's sharper than the big one'. I said I thought he was saying he was sharper than me and he grinned. He turned the pencil and the lead broke off. He seemed surprised, open-mouthed. He watched the sharpenings fall to the floor and showed me the 'sharp point'. When it was really sharp he jumped about, grinning, excited. I said that he seemed excited and he touched it with a finger tip, slightly pressing it in. He offered me 'a feel'. I said 'No — I don't need to.' He said 'It's not all that sharp'. He said 'It's little, then it's big, then it's little again', holding the pencil below the level of the chair seat and saying that it has something to do with the light (perhaps a reference to something magic, like a penis becoming erect, not understood by Robert and maybe seen as something like a trick of the light). He looked at the lead on his hands and asked if he needed to wash them. I said I thought he was worried about dirt, about something dirty and he said 'where's the lorry?'

He then moved beside me (the two chairs were side by side) and went through 'What my little sister does', sliding over the chair frontwards to the floor. He then acted as though he was trying to climb on to the chair then put his cheek against the chair and pretended to be asleep. He got up and stumbled, nearly diving head first down the small gap between the chairs.

He stood by me and looked in the box and picked out the glue stick. He looked at me, puzzled, and said 'What is it?' He took off the lid and seemed intrigued and perhaps excited by propelling it out. Again he talked about it being little then big. He rewound it and invited me to look inside but then put it down and went back over to the telephone box. He traced the tube that connected the two phones and said that there was something inside. He sat down in the box and proceeded to spit down the receiver, shaking it and intently watching the spit trickle down the tube. He drew my attention to it, holding it up for me to see. He said he wanted something for the coin slot and came over to pick up the sellotape. He put it down the slot and seemed pleased that it went through.

Then, towards the end of the 50 minute session:

I said we had five minutes left. He began sellotaping around the slot, flicking bits of sellotape on to the floor, seemingly oblivious of this. He asked 'How many minutes?' I replied 'Four'. He stuck the sellotape roll to the inside of the telephone box. He picked up the police car and found the ambulance and sped it across the table. It was time to finish. He had seemingly been oblivious to my requests to tidy up and I thought he would refuse to leave. He wheeled the two vehicles over the chair beside me then put them both down on the table. I said I would put them back in the box for next time. He clutched one to him, crossly, saying he would not be allowed back. He would not be coming again, his 'foster mother' would not come again. I said it was time to finish. He let me take the car from him and put it in the box. He walked quickly out of the room back to his foster mother, climbed on to the rocking horse and started to rock furiously, very 'high' and excited.

What had this first session revealed? First of all, that clinical supervision was required — and most of this work was supervised by Shirley Truckle, NSPCC regional advisor and principal child psychotherapist. Her supervision was not only to help me to understand Robert's communications more fully and to pull out themes of concern, but also to help me with my anxieties. Robert was an unnerving child to be with. I often left the sessions feeling quite shaken by him. At the time I thought the other team members found this hard to relate to but, in fact, they were finding it hard to know what to do. There seemed to be new rules about confidentiality. Did these extend to asking me about sessions and offering support? Would that be breaching confidentiality? We did manage to sort out these tensions and misunderstandings, some of which were about getting to know one another — which takes time too — but also to do with the style of working. Intense feelings can be stirred up and this can lead to clashes and even civil wars amongst teams and networks! Most seriously, when working with such deprived clients, many forms of support become necessary and vital — close supervision definitely and, if possible, some personal therapy or at least, sympathetic and supportive colleagues who can help with thinking about the emotional experience.

In this first session, Robert seemed to be showing me how he was a bright and alert child who related in a superficial and disconnected way but displayed enormous need. He appeared genuinely thrown by my noticing what he did and even more non-plussed by my making any sense of it, whether it was right or not. Most of the time I felt we did not share a common language. He repeated activities as if for the first time. It was as though he was showing how nothing seemed to 'stick', nothing had a place where it belonged, there was no reference point. His play seemed sexualized, angry and excited. He appeared to relate to me, ask me questions and direct talk my way but it felt so superficial and somehow unreachable. It is the kind of experience that can make you feel you are crazy, when what is seen and said does not match up with, or is a gulf apart, from what is felt.

The next three sessions added weight to this. It became evident that beneath the mask of bright activity, Robert was a frightened child who trusted no-one and was very confused about how to relate to anyone, except in a 'chocolate boxy', sexualized way. So many of his play situations conveyed a sense of great precariousness but with no awareness of this expressed by himself or anyone else (I know that was not actually the case; many people were concerned, but as far as Robert saw it, no-one noticed. He had no expectation of being protected and anyway, as he saw it, whatever seemed good got spoilt). This was really a picture of a child who had taken in very little experience of being parented, of being looked out for, of someone responding to his needs. No doubt his youthful parents had had to struggle as hard as they could to keep themselves ticking over let alone having any spare capacity to cope with a new baby in stressful family and living circumstances. Robert was disturbed and frightened and most of the time worryingly disconnected from these, if not from all, feelings. That meant he did not form real relationships with people (confirmed by his foster mother), that he didn't particularly care for or look after himself, and that he expected feelings to be thrown back at him. So for him the world was an unsafe place, where little should or could be divulged to others or to himself in ways that would allow something to be done about it. To quote from session 5:

> Robert proceeded to bury himself under the beanbags, saying something to that effect as he did so. He then became silent. It was a very full silence. I spoke to him of the many things he felt he had to keep hidden from me and from other people, keeping them out of sight. I could then hear a faint clicking sound and wondered what he might be doing. I suddenly thought that there might be an electric socket buried beneath the beanbags and thought he might be trying to pick off one of the child protection covers. I then thought that there was no such cover and thought he might be switching it on and off and sticking his fingers in the socket. I got up went over to him, telling him what I was doing because I thought he wasn't safe. His head emerged and he grinned up at me. As he moved, the beanbag was pushed aside to reveal a double electric socket, without safety covers. Looking up at me he switched the switch on and off. He then slowly traced one of the holes with his finger, almost pushing his finger inside. I said that touching electric sockets like that was very dangerous, he could be really hurt. He grinned up at me and stopped. I spoke to him of how dangerous he might feel everything was at the moment and perhaps he was wondering did anyone notice, would anyone notice? Then, quite seriously, he asked if I would call the police. I talked to him about needing someone who would notice and help him to control what he was doing, feeling that he needed someone to notice and help. I spoke to him about why, when I noticed what dangerous things were going on, I was still only seeing him for such a short time and told him that we had today's and another session left. He asked what the time was and I told him there were 35 minutes left.

Then, to quote from a sequence a few minutes later:

> Robert got up and walked over to the chair on the opposite side of the room. He clambered over it and ended up standing on his head. He then got up and proceeded to climb over the back

of the chair, standing astride, one leg on the floor. He did this twice. He then attempted to climb the shelves, putting one foot on the lower shelf and putting his weight on it. I went over to him and said that was not a safe thing to do. He said 'Yes, it is!' and proceeded to put his weight on the next shelf up. I said I didn't want him to get hurt, that there was a risk of him getting hurt. He looked up at me with surprise and said 'I miss my Dad', then, 'My Mum would hurt me if I went back'. He seemed real at this point and puzzled and cross. I talked to him about how there was so much going on in his life, about where people lived and what was going to happen to him that might seem very wobbly and unsafe and very difficult for him. He clambered back on to the chair and looked out of the window. He started making noises. He grinned at me and said he was barking like a dog. This bark then changed into a long howl and I said that noise sounded very sad. He looked at me and said 'No, it isn't!' and then proceeded to make a tiny little sound, like a baby. I said that sounded like a cry and Robert retorted 'No!'. I then said it sounded like a little noise and he agreed. He looked down the long garden and whispered to me that there was a monster outside, could I see it in the garden? I talked to him about how he might feel there were all sorts of monsters around him when so much seemed unsafe and out of control. In a rather excited fashion Robert started to talk about this 'monster'. I asked him what it looked like. He moved very close to me, holding a small sponge ball and a length of plastic he had found amongst the beanbags. There seemed to be something malevolent about the way he made his approach. I was ready to move quickly, if I needed to. I thought he might be about to poke me in the eye. He passed by me to the beanbags and, in a hushed voice, said he had to hide. He half hid himself amongst the beanbags, still stage-whispering about the monster. I talked to him about how he might feel the room was a rather dangerous place to be in, full of all sorts of scarey thoughts and feelings. He then got out of the beanbags and said to me, in a rather earnest and needy way, that he wanted to go to the toilet. I think he felt everything was getting too much and going to the loo was one way of letting things out and flushing them away.

Once again Robert was playing out his own emotional disconnection from disturbing and dangerous events. He did not expect me to notice danger or act on his behalf to keep him safe and was very surprised when I did. He couldn't bear to see what he himself did for more than a few seconds at a time, so he would deny everything he had done or what was going on — not lying but *having* to deny what went on, which was hardly surprising, in view of all his experiences.

Then a few paragraphs from the last session, session 6:

> My first sight of Robert was him kneeling on his foster mother's lap, grinning and apparently pummelling her. As he came with me to the room he stopped and grinned over to his foster mother, saying 'Do I look nice?', displaying his yellow T-shirt. He began to tuck it in his trousers rather laboriously. His foster mother replied 'Yes' then he ran over to her and loved her in a very 'chocolate boxy' way. He then waved back at her in a theatrical manner.

Then a minute into the session:

> He began to rummage in the box and picked up an unopened box of plasticine. He looked at it for a second then flung it back as though it had given him a shock or was highly repellent. He turned to me, saying earnestly 'Can I go to the toilet?
>
> When he returned — his foster mother took him to the loo — he picked up the plasticine and fingered the ridges through the polythene window. He looked up at me, puzzled, and asked 'Is this plasticine or crayon? I asked him what he thought. He asked me again. I said he didn't seem at all sure what things were, what they really were, so could he trust anything by what it looked like? He opened the packet and frowned 'It's plasticine'. He banged it vertically, quite hard on the table, several times. He then started to separate the different coloured strips and thoughtfully dropped one into the box then another. I said he seemed to be telling me about separation, being pulled away then just dropped. I said this was our last session — number six of six — and maybe this felt like being dropped too. I felt sad and said parting might be sad for him too. He dropped the rest of the strips into the box with increasing conviction. He dismissively threw the plasticine's wrappings and the emptied felt pen pack over the other side of the table, onto the floor. He picked up a shallow basket, examined it, then threw that over

the table onto the floor, in a knowing way. He picked up an empty jar with the lid screwed on and examined it thoughtfully. He then put it back in the box. He looked miffed and angry. I said I though he was angry with me for ending with him, dropping him, a feeling he had probably had before. He picked up two strips of plasticine, the brown and the red, and went round the corner, just out of sight and started hurling these strips against the wall opposite. He picked up all the strips and repeated his hurling. I said I thought he was showing me how angry he was, like he was being knocked about against a brick wall. He threw with increasing ferocity, crowing as he managed to hit the wall-mounted microphone. I felt very intimidated — in the firing line and caught in the crossfire, especially when one piece of plasticine flew at an angle across the room, a few feet from my face. I was on the verge of deciding that this was becoming unsafe. I also felt caught, unable to manoeuvre with Robert out of view. I said I thought he was letting me know what it was like to be in the firing line, feeling things were being thrown at him, feeling it was dangerous and there was nothing he could do about it — like so many things that were happening at the moment — with school and his foster parents. He resumed his throwing but more calmly. Then, for some reason, I took my mind off him. I turned round to see Robert peering from around the corner, poised to throw a piece of plasticine at me. I said I thought he needed someone to notice and pay attention to what he was doing. More ferocious throwing at the wall. I said I thought he was wanting all the upset and worry to stop. He then calmed a little, saying he was aiming for the beanbags in the corner. He successfully landed a few bits on a particular beanbag. One brown bit went wide, off target, and fell to the floor. I said I thought he was saying how he wanted to be collected up, gathered together somewhere comfortable and soft, instead of being so knocked and thrown about. He responded by marching up to the beanbags, saying with his back to me 'No, I don't!' He rummaged down the back of the beanbags, picking up a few pieces of plasticine, then nestled himself in the bags, placing one bag over his lap.

Then there was more throwing of plasticine at a picture of two children, just above my shoulder. A piece hit. I said I thought he was telling me how even though things were not aimed at him, they got near to him and could hurt him too. I decided I was being too vague, so said 'like with Lee'. (There had been a very recent crisis with Lee, leading to his removal from the foster home). He immediately stopped what he was doing, looking deep in thought, then said laughing with contempt — 'Lee, he's gone, he's gone to another foster home — you don't know anything — you're wrong!' I said 'I know Lee has been moved and that makes you feel things — even though you haven't been moved you still feel things about it'. He started to collect pieces of plasticine from the floor and suddenly dumped them in a pile beneath the radiator, exclaiming with surprise and disgust 'shit'. He ran over to the coffee table and said 'I haven't done her (his foster mother's) picture.

By the end of the session Robert had become increasingly exasperated, arrogant and excited. After he had left, I returned to the room. It seemed that everything was loose, their containing packets thrown aside. The crayons were loose on the table, their box thrown by the beanbags, the cardboard insides removed. There were bits and pieces of plasticine all over the place. I felt like lying down somewhere soft and quiet for an hour myself. I felt distraught and wrung out.

Robert had shown me something of the taunting, teasing and aggressive world he perceived and had conveyed a feeling of being a puppet on a string.

The actual experience of having been with Robert proved to be invaluable in two crises which broke during the assessment period.

The social worker telephoned us to let us know that Robert was about to be excluded from school. Su and I decided to handle this by arranging to meet with the Deputy Head and Robert's class teacher. We had deliberated over who should go — if I went would that be breaching boundaries? — but finally decided we needed each other's support so we went together. I think the situation was held together by my being able to describe, on the basis of the information gained from the exploratory session, how Robert made others feel — that is: impotent, as though one is speaking a foreign language to him. I described how he deleted from his mind what he had done or asked, literally a few seconds earlier, and how often I felt on the edge of my seat, ready for danger. That was just how the Class Teacher felt, being driven up the wall with no hope of being able to do anything about it. Of course, the teacher knew he had many resources — his own experience, the support of the school's Deputy Head — but somehow Robert's impact was to make the teacher feel he had nothing to fall back on, that he had no control, and did not expect to have any influence. By the end of the meeting, fortunately, the school decided to plough on and we really felt we were working as a team, in partnership.

The second crisis occurred the day before the final exploratory session. Robert and Lee, the older foster child were found in bed together by one of the foster parents' adult relations. Robert had apparently invited Lee into his bed to 'do what he's done before' and Lee had done so, saying he was magic and would make Robert warm. Lee was removed quickly from the home. Su met with the foster mother, who was very shaken and distressed by the speed of reaction. That was probably a notable time when the network did break down or become ineffective, aggravated by our own unavailability at the time and the fact that people were just about to go on leave.

As the exploration sessions progressed and crises were dealt with, the equally crucial work of meeting with Robert's foster carers continued. This reveals another angle, separate but linked, to the exploration sessions but which is best followed through from beginning to end. It is written from the worker's, Su Beech's, perspective.

Robert had been living for 18 months with Jackie and Derrick, a couple in their fifties who were very experienced parents and foster carers. The household comprised the couple, their two adult daughters, an adopted son (15), and foster children Lee (11), Robert, and a three year old girl and her baby sister.

The couple had a commitment to care for Lee and Robert long term, but were in the process of a rehabilitation of the two younger children to their natural parents. As well as the seven young people, there were three large dogs, four cats, and a cage of hamsters. Jackie's elderly father also lived with the family and during the course of our work had a bad fall, fracturing his femur and aggravating a diabetic condition that caused him to become vague and confused. He was also aphasic.

My first visit to the home was with the family's linkworker and the purpose was for me to be introduced and talk to the family about the workers' meeting and the nature of the work that was being suggested. I discussed the reasons we had not invited them to this meeting, and this did not seem to be a problem. Jackie also seemed to have a good understanding of why it would be important for Robert to know that what he said would not be

65

passed on to herself or others unless there were child protection implications. We arranged a pattern of regular contact during the course of Robert's assessment. My brief with Jackie was to give them space to think about Robert, about themselves in relation to him, and to look at any impact that the work he was doing at The Elms was having at home. It was very possible that the work would have an effect that could be perceived as 'detrimental': if Robert realised that someone might really help him think about what his experiences had meant to him, might really try to understand what it was like to be him, he might well become more upset, and his behaviour more difficult. I was not there to assess them as appropriate carers for Robert, and I offered them confidentiality — I would feed back to Social Services Department only what they wanted to share, unless there were child protection issues.

During the work with Jackie and Derrick several important issues emerged. At the start I was told that the couple were hoping to foster Robert long term and had a great commitment to him. They said that the social worker had told them how important they were to Robert, and he had been told that he would stay with them. They said that when he came to them he had few social skills: he did not know how to use a knife and fork, and had no idea how to play. They had, they said, persisted with him and seen real progress. They stressed the positive aspects of caring for Robert — he was very physically affectionate, he had learned basic skills, all agreed that he had 'come on' considerably with the love and care they were able to offer.

Gradually however, another picture emerged — it appeared important for me to acknowledge how hard they were working for Robert and how small the 'improvements' seemed to be. They spoke of his 'strangeness': how he would sit for ages 'pulling faces to himself', and playing with his fingers or masturbating; how he was so much slower than their three year old grandchild, seeming unable to make connections and act spontaneously; how even his speech was slow and laboured — his favourite phrase 'I don't know' seeming to reflect that he was indeed living in a different world; how he was clumsy, showing a lack of awareness of the world around him and the effect he had on it.

From my social work training and by inclination, I felt the need to reassure them, to be positive about the progress that was being made, and to acknowledge how progress was bound to be slow.

However, I felt it was essential to resist this desire and I stayed with their discomfort and took up their negative feelings. As I acknowledged how hard this must be to cope with, Jackie moved on to say how painful it was to her to believe that she could not 'love a five year old better'. She was also beginning to feel that the very thing she felt she and her family could provide for children — love and care — were the things that Robert just couldn't accept, couldn't use, and which might indeed make him more aware of himself as a 'different' unlovable child.

This was extremely painful to Jackie who prided herself on a long and successful fostering career, coping with difficult children and 'never giving up'. Thinking seriously about the possibility of Robert needing to live in a different environment put her in touch with feelings of loss she'd experienced when a child had been removed from her care after five years because she was black and considered to need a same-race placement.

Equally difficult for Jackie was accepting that she was actually finding it very hard to love Robert. She experienced a feeling of being held permanently at arm's length: Robert's display of physical affection lacked depth and he made her feel hopeless as a parent, unable to make real emotional contact with him, and unsure 'what to say and do for the best'.

She was able to say that she actually found him very uncomfortable to be with at times. His sexuality, the way he would look at other children, made her edgy and watchful. She concocted elaborate and quite unrealistic schemes to prevent him from being alone with other children, because of her fears that he might have sexual contact with them or be spiteful towards them. She was very frightened that he might engage in sexual activity with Lee who, it was suspected, had himself been sexually abused: she would feel particularly responsible for Robert as she had been central to the process which induced him to disclose that he had been sexually abused in another foster home. Consequently he would feel she had really betrayed him if it happened again in her home and she also felt that she would be criticised by the Department.

During the course of the work the two boys did engage in sexual activity and Lee was rapidly removed. This highlighted for Jackie the fact that although Lee had only been with them for a comparatively short time, she had a closer relationship with him than with Robert. It also brought her face to face with the fact that she was potentially facing enormous loss: her father was ill and talking about dying; Lee had left; the two younger children, one of whom she had fostered for three years from infancy, were about to move back home; and she was reaching the conclusion that her home was not the most appropriate place for Robert.

The information she had given us about Robert and the quality of his relationships within the family was of enormous importance and confirmed much of what was becoming evident in the assessment. Because her discomfort was taken very seriously she was able to shift perceptibly in her own feelings about caring for Robert and was more able to concentrate on his needs and the difficulty of meeting such enormous needs in the context of

* her own family. She was able to feel this less as a failure on the part of herself and her family, which had been a major factor in her thinking, and more as a positive statement that needed to be made in the context of planning for Robert's future.*

Clearly this was all crucial information for those charged with making decisions for Robert. I am not suggesting that the network were unaware of the issues that the couple were raising, but it did seem that the size of the problem that Robert presented in the family might possibly have been minimised within the context of a Department strapped for resources and a family who set great store by being able to cope with whatever problems needy children presented.

The family were identifying issues on which they needed specific help from the Department. They wanted to make their feelings about caring for Robert on a long term basis clear in the context of a fuller understanding of Robert's needs. They wanted to think further about Lee and his removal from their home — to think about his possible rehabilitation or at least a structure in which to have contact with him and to think and talk about their separation, so as to help both him and Robert to make sense of it. They were aware that their feelings about 'losing' Robert were located within strong feelings of loss and threatened loss, and they needed space to mourn.

I, too, learned a great deal from this piece of work. I found myself having to rethink boundaries. Where does support become assessment? I was not there to assess them as carers, but certainly formed a clear idea that this was not an appropriate long-term placement for Robert. When does 'thinking' become therapy? It would have been impossible and inappropriate to offer therapy within the confines of this short-term work but there were times when therapeutic needs were evident, and times when our relationship was used by Jackie to sort our her feelings about other parts of the network.

I was reminded again of the enormous expectations we have of foster carers: Jackie brought Robert for sessions each week but received no direct feedback on his sessions. What really happened in that Therapy Room? Jackie and Derrick inevitably felt threatened by this process, and indeed by the fact that there was so much concern about Robert: was this a reflection on their parenting? On their family? Were they being criticised for putting the needs of their other children before Robert? Why was he not improving after 18 months? Jackie felt that the basic problem for Robert was that he simply was not wanted by his parents — she felt that this must be at the root of his difficulties: was what she was feeling yet another rejection of him?

Foster carers have an extremely difficult task in even the most straight-forward situations, and there is enormous pressure on field social workers and foster carers to maintain placements. Jackie and Derrick were receiving excellent support from their linkworker and from the community social worker, but it did seem very important that there was also this support from a project worker: the assessment process would do nothing to make a very difficult situation any easier; on the contrary it was stressful and probably threatening. Someone connected with the project needed to hold this anxiety within the network, so that they could work to help Robert survive the process.

It seemed by the end of the process that there was a very solid alliance amongst the workers who had the most direct contact with Robert — foster carers, school, The Elms, the social worker — and all were acknowledging the depth of his need. I was left particularly with great respect for Jackie and Derrick, who were able to think so sensitively about Robert's needs in the midst of so many competitive demands.

To return to Robert and the report-writing stage. Team discussions had to take place about the report's contents — how much detail should be given, how much was necessary? Discussion had to bring together the two line management and clinical management systems — the child protection and the child psychotherapy systems — and take account of the Children Act, child protection issues and child psychotherapy points of view. This all went ahead even though time was scarce and diaries were not easy to juggle.

It was decided, amicably, that the report should not go into the session details, in order to respect Robert's confidentiality. Instead, impressions were given — his fright, his panic, his disconnection and perhaps most importantly how people with Robert might feel — not so much how he made people feel, which would imply some kind of blame — but his way of virtually pushing his feelings of chaos, impotence, exasperation into other people so that they feel *they* are the ones going up the wall. I am not normally terrified of being harmed, poked in the eye and intruded upon by a 5 year old, whom I could easily manage physically if absolutely necessary. So that was a real clue to his experience of danger often looming, of being poked into and invaded.

Due directly to the level and quality of Robert's disturbance, the team decided to recommend placement in a therapeutic community, where Robert's emotional difficulties could be attended to as well as his educational needs. We were of the opinion that it was unlikely that any foster placement or ordinary school would be able to manage and help Robert in the long term. He did not really attach to people, he was a likely risk to other children in a family and if/or when he did get in touch with how awful he felt, it could well be like all hell breaking loose. As a team, we doubted whether any family would be able to manage all this. So it was against the odds we decided to push for therapeutic community placement; a recommendation to which the social worker added considerable effort.

Another issue that was bubbling away in the background was when, to whom and how to feed our report back. Since we had recommended placement in a therapeutic community, a very expensive option in the short term (though not in the long term if one considers the cost of social work time, residential care, or even, to look on the bleak side, the expense of maintaining someone in prison), it was essential for Robert that the network did act together otherwise there would be no hope of success. A statutory review needed to be arranged and the social worker suggested we give our feedback there.

It was true that everyone would be present, but we were keen for all parties to be working together as well as possible before that all important decision-making review.

This meant setting up a series of meetings, with appropriate combinations of people, with appropriate levels of privacy and time to think.

Naturally our first meeting had to be with Robert's social worker. Because of the difficult situation over the removal of the other foster child and some questioning of our wish to present our report to a series of meetings rather than providing the statutory review, we arranged a meeting with the social worker, his Team Leader, the social worker for the older foster child (Lee), our Team Manager and Su and myself. In the event it was a meeting between the social worker and ourselves. The report had been sent to the social worker beforehand and the meeting provided a good opportunity for further questions and clarification. He recognised the Robert described in the report and agreed with our conclusions about the level of Robert's disturbance and with the recommendation of therapeutic community placement. The issues about feedback after each session still rattled around but in discussing it further it became clear that the social worker had felt rather uncertain about explaining the whole procedure to Robert's parents and managing their considerable anxieties about their son and his future when it was a new experience for him. We put forward our plan on how to feed back to the rest of the network. Our plan was as follows::

1. Su and the linkworker would meet with Robert's foster parents and take the report with them (we were against the idea of reports landing on doorsteps without anyone there to explain or help with the upset). We thought the foster carers might like to have agreed minutes taken of this meeting so that their views could be represented at the review, in writing. As it turned out they were very pleased to do this as was the linkworker. Of course, the report was discussed with the linkworker too, prior to this meeting.

2. The social worker, the Family Centre worker who met regularly with Robert's parents, and Su would meet with Robert's parents, again taking the report along with them. A second meeting was arranged for further discussion after Robert's mother and father had had a chance to think matters over.

3. Su and I would meet with the school personnel and the Educational Psychologist, the report having been posted to all parties beforehand.

This plan sought to ensure that everyone in the network had a chance to read and consider the same report before the review, where decisions would be made and definite action plans drawn up.

Fortunately the meetings went very well. Robert's parents were upset but not shocked. His mother said she recognised much of herself in her son and knew she couldn't look after him. They maintained this view in the second, pre-arranged meeting.

The statutory review followed very shortly after these meetings. It was decided, again after a fair amount of thrashing out that I, as the child's therapist, would not attend. The therapist's role would be protected, as would Robert's confidentiality. Our team manager and Su attended and again all parties felt adequately prepared, considered and able to put their points of view. It was independently chaired and everyone at the meeting was congratulated on the productive way in which it was conducted — as working very much in the child's interests. There had been no surprises, which is not to say it was stage-managed but simply that everyone had had a chance to think about and react to the report's contents and recommendations beforehand.

More reviews ensued. There was a change of foster placement for Robert. Robert's poor behaviour had been blamed, in most people's view quite erroneously, on his foster carers and they felt unable to manage an already 'sinking ship' any longer. Several further letters had to be written, backing up our recommendation and arguing against other options. Further assessment was requested since Robert was behaving so well at his next (and sixth) foster placement. Could it be that he was really less disturbed and no longer in need of special care? This question was answered with a resounding 'no'. We felt it more likely that Robert was giving up, that, more worryingly, he was retreating into a shell rather than making people sit up and notice. We also felt that to expect Robert to open up another time for us to watch him bleed was too much — one form of institutional abuse.

Finally, one year later Robert was granted funding for a therapeutic community and the best placement was sought and secured by the social worker. This is hardly a fairy tale ending, but most definitely an example of two different cultures — child protection and child psychotherapy — coming together, appreciating their differences and similarities, and working together to ensure the work remained child-centred, so that no-one, especially not the child, would fall through the caring professions' safety net.

Further Reading
Boston, M and Szur, R (eds) (1983), *Psychotherapy with severely Deprived Children*, London, Maresfield Library

6
Multi-professionalism: the role of the family

Kate Morris

Introduction

Family Rights Group (FRG) is a national charity which aims to improve the law and practice concerning families and children in need of local authority services or involved in child protection procedures. We offer an advice and advocacy service to individual families, and information and training for professionals involved in working with families. It is, in particular, experiences and information from families using the advice service that inform this chapter.

The following considers the role of families within multi-professionalism, focusing particularly on child protection procedures. It argues that, despite the Children Act 1989 and the revised *Working Together* guidance (Department of Health 1991), families too often remain outside looking in when child protection concerns lead to professional involvement.

In the chapter brief consideration is given to the recent history of the relationship between families and professionals. Some of the current experiences of families are explored, with reference to the inequalities facing families as a result of racism and discrimination. In conclusion new developments are discussed and ways forward considered.

It is useful in this complex area to define some of the terms. The term 'family' refers here to all family adults members — children, adults, and extended family members. Each individual family will have its own definition of what constitutes a family member and therefore a rigid definition is unhelpful. The term multi-professionalism is defined as joint action by a number of individual professionals from different disciplines towards a common aim.

73

Finally we adopt the following definition for partnership:

the essence of partnership is sharing. It is marked by respect for one another, role divisions, right to information, accountability, competence and value accorded to individual input. In short each partner is seen as having something to contribute, power is shared, decisions are made jointly, and roles are not only respected but also backed by legal and moral rights (Tunnard 1992).

Families and Professionals

The 1950s and 1960s heralded recognition of the 'battered child' syndrome and the development of a model of professional involvement that was based on treating and nurturing families back to health. Families were perceived as essentially protective, and failure to be so was argued to be linked to the stress and strains of parenting. However the Marie Colwell Inquiry, (Department of Health and Social Security 1974), and subsequent child death inquiries, provoked public outcry that professionals were doing too little too late. Professionals' perceptions of families began to shift. Concepts of 'dangerous' and 'taking control' began to come into professional use, and the 1970s showed a significant increase in the use of place of safety orders. (Parton, 1991).

In the 1980s research started to provide evidence that the professional approach of making decisions for the family without necessarily informing and involving them was unhelpful and at times damaging. In addition the use of emergency powers not only caused the family trauma (in particular the child) but was also shown to result in poor planning and difficulties for families in maintaining contact with each other (Parton 1991). Evidence showed that, once in the care system, family members lost touch and inadequate plans meant children became 'lost in care' (Millham et al 1986).

The events in Cleveland and the subsequent inquiry report (Butler Sloss 1988) identified other problems, and public criticism centred on professionals being seen as over-zealous and unnecessarily intrusive into family life. Meanwhile the research evidence showed that medium to long-term professional input was often associated with inadequate support for families. It also highlighted that parents still had an important contribution to make their children's well-being even if the child could not live with them (Department of Health 1991). Consequently professional approaches to permanency that were based on a 'clean break' were not necessarily in the child's best interests.

The Children Act 1989 drew on much of this research. It demanded a shift in professional attitudes away from decision-making for families by professionals who 'knew best'. Instead the principles of the Act expect that families should be partners in the planning processes. This is firmly underlined in the volumes of guidance to the Act. Use of emergency powers and compulsory intervention are constrained both by the Act's requirements for partnership and by the no order principle.

The current edition of *Working Together* reflects the expectation that professionals should recognise families as partners when developing their practice and procedures:

> Agencies should ensure that staff who are concerned with the protection of children from abuse understand that this assumption in the Act of a high degree of co-operation between parents and local authorities requires a concerted approach to inter-disciplinary and inter-agency working (DoH, 1991, Paragraph 1.7).

Both the Children Act and *Working Together* recognise that neither professionals nor families alone keep children safe — but that by working in partnership children's needs will be best met.

In summary, professional understanding of, and attitudes towards the role of families in child protection has changed significantly during the last three decades. Families, from being perceived as in need of professional care and treatment, became 'objects of concern' and, most recently, potential partners in keeping children safe.

Family Experiences

Family experiences of professional involvement cannot easily be summarised, given the range of child care practice. The following therefore identifies some examples of current practice and their implications for partnership. Specifically, child protection procedures, as recommended in *Working Together* and implemented by Area Child Protection Committees, are considered.

Department of Health statistics show that some 80 per cent of children currently registered on the child protection registers live at home. (Department of Health 1993). For these children their day to day safety rests largely with the adult family members. For the protection plan to be effective in respect of these children, the family members must contribute to, understand and agree the plans the child protection conference has produced. *Working Together* also makes clear the expectation that family members be present throughout the conference unless exceptional circumstances apply.

> While there may be exceptional occasions when it will not be right to invite one or other parent to attend a case conference in whole or in part, exclusion should be kept to a minimum and needs to be especially justified (DoH, 1991, Paragraph 6.15).

Despite this guidance and the statistics, some Area Child Protection Committees continue to stipulate mandatory exclusion of the family members from certain parts of the conference. Usually this includes the discussion of risk, registration and protection plans. Families therefore continue to face real barriers to partnership — understanding and implementing a plan the family has not helped to design is particularly difficult. Research also shows that partial attendance for families is of limited usefulness and can have the same effect on the family as total exclusion. (Thoburn, forthcoming).

The same procedures that automatically exclude family members from parts of the conference provide guidance on network abuse, institutional abuse, and extra-family abuse. This illustrates that the expanding professional knowledge of the complexities of child protection does not necessarily go hand in hand with increased family participation and partnership. The increasingly sophisticated professional knowledge base can leave the fundaments of partnership with families unaddressed. Therefore for the family the emphasis on multi-professionalism can be a marginalising experience.

The right of families to disagree or complain about the services they receive is codified in the Children Act. Similar rights in respect of child protection services and procedures are not necessarily recognised in the local Area Child Protection Committee guidelines, although they are recommended in *Working Together*. Families express considerable frustration that there is no national and often no local agreed process for their voice to be heard. Professionals afford each other the procedural opportunities to disagree on decisions regarding registration and, by representation on Area Child Protection Committees, the ability to consider and challenge other agencies' practices. Such opportunities are vital in ensuring that the multi-professional practice evolves effectively. However, without routes for consumer feedback and involvement in service design, families cannot be partners in this multi-professional process.

Historically professional understanding of child protection has been based on a white Euro-centric view of families. One result is that protection issues such as racist assaults on children have not generally been addressed in local child protection procedures. The lack of consultation in designing services has meant that for black families the procedures and the services do not necessarily reflect their needs or concerns. Similarly, the procedures struggle to meet the needs of families with individual members who are disabled or lesbian or gay.

If the knowledge and skills in multi-professional practice increase, without issues of partnership and anti-oppressive practice being addressed, families' experience of discrimination and oppression can be reinforced.

The examples considered here are illustrative of the difficulties in achieving partnership with families, without attitudinal change. The right of families to be included in multi-professional developments and strategies is dependent on professionals perceiving positively the contributions families can make. It also rests on professional understanding about the limits of their roles. While the framework provided by the Children Act and *Working Together* acknowledges the central role of partnership, family experiences of child protection policy and procedures has yet to reflect this.

Ways Forward

As described, partnership in child protection challenges both professional attitudes and practice. If partnership is to be achieved families cannot be judged to have rights dependent on their 'innocence' or 'guilt'. It is difficult to accept the positive elements which occurred, yet research shows that, in terms of a child's future well-being, professionals must recognise and preserve a child's connections to their family members.

Child protection, is, perhaps, the most difficult arena in which to develop consumer involvement. However, failure to do so, as past experience and research evidence shows, can lead to ineffective protection plans and disenfranchised families. There follows an account of two practice developments that specifically aim to empower families in child protection services. As partnership continues to be explored by professionals such developments provide opportunities to progress the expectations of both the Children Act 1989 and *Working Together*.

Family membership of Area Child Protection Committees

Area Child Protection Committees (ACPC) can be experienced by both families and professionals as remote, often unknown, unapproachable and seemingly unaccountable committees. This can create a wide gap between the procedures adopted by ACPC and the actual child protection practice. Yet the ACPC will be crucial in, for example, the development of a Complaint and Appeals Procedure for families. Similarly, the commitment of the ACPC to equal opportunities and anti-oppressive practices will generate child protection services that families find far more accessible and relevant. Such developments by ACPCs will need consumer comment and involvement — they cannot be designed effectively in a vacuum.

Family Rights Group is aware of ACPCs which have family representatives as members. This development creates a climate in which true partnership can flourish. The growing number of active self-help groups for families offer professionals the opportunity to recruit such family representatives. This is not an easy development and careful preparation and support for family members is necessary but the benefits are considerable both for the professionals providing the service and for the families receiving it.

Working Together also recommends that ACPCs establish links with other related agencies, such as voluntary organisations who provide relevant services and organisations who represent religious or cultural interests. By doing so the ACPC could begin to bridge the gaps between policies, procedures and local needs.

Family Group Conferences

Family Group Conferences originated in New Zealand. This model has the extended family as the primary planning group. The professional role is one of information and knowledge-sharing and, where necessary, of mediator.

In this model professionals provide families with information and knowledge at a family meeting, then withdraw from the meeting to allow the family to discuss and plan in private.

If, and only if, the family and professionals cannot agree a plan and the child/children are felt to be at significant risk, does the matter go before the court.

In New Zealand the adoption nationally of this model of practice via recent legislation led to an 80 per cent drop in the in-care population, with only approximately 2 per cent of cases being referred to the court for a decision.

In the United Kingdom several local authorities and a voluntary agency are piloting the use of Family Group Conferences. This development has generated much professional debate, as roles shift from expert decision-maker to that of mediator/facilitator. Personal and professional values and attitudes are challenged when families assume such a powerful role. However, experiences indicate that families produce plans which professionals readily accept and in the process of doing so, families deal with many issues professionals find it difficult to broach.

Conclusion

Families' experiences of multi-professional involvement can often be alienating and disempowering. Whilst professionals may have the framework for partnership the development of multi-agency practice does not necessarily reflect this. Families can continue to be marginalised in decision making and planning processes. Similarly families are under-represented or poorly consulted in the design of services or procedures.

Families report the lack of written and verbal information and a professional approach that sees them as attenders rather than participants in the process. Families also continue to feel frustrated by the use of jargon and feelings that there are hidden agendas. Racism and discrimination can create further barriers for families.

All these features can be addressed and changed by the professionals involved. The concern expressed in this chapter is that multi-professionalism does not always focus on the development of these partnership skills. Whilst attitudinal change may be slow, the two developments in policy and practice discussed here illustrate that professionals are, in some areas, grasping the challenge partnership presents. Multi-professionalism, if developed within a commitment to partnership, can offer innovative and informed services.

Ultimately the development of multi-professional approaches to child protection can only be useful if the families involved feel better able to protect children. Professionals will only know this if families are given an equal voice and role in the decision-making processes.

References

Department of Health and social Security (1974) *Marie Coldwell Inquiry* London, HMSO.

Department of Health (1991) *Working Together Under the Children Act 1989 — A Guide to Arrangements for Inter-Agency Cooperation for the Protection of Children from abuse* London, HMSO.

Department of Health (1991) *Patterns and Outcomes in Child Placement: Messages from Current Research and Their Implications* London, HMSO.

Department of Health (1993) *Children and Young people on Child Protection Registers — Year Ending 31 March 1992, England: Provisional Feedback* London, HMSO.

Parton, N. (1991) *Governing the Family — Child Care, Child Protection and the State* London, Macmillan.

Thoburn, J. (forthcoming) Norwich, University of East Anglia.

Tunnard, J. (1992) *Setting the Scene for Partnership: The Children Act 1989: Working in Partnership with Families* London, Family Rights Group.

7
Training teachers in child protection: Initial Teacher Education

Rosalind Goodyear

Initial teacher education has changed considerably over the past fifteen years. The change can be traced ostensibly to James Callaghan's Ruskin speech of 1975 which became, post hoc, the start of the Great Debate, and to a government White Paper, *Better Schools* (1985). From then on, the government of the day has taken a keen and active interest in all levels of education, culminating in the *Education Reform Act* of 1988 and the Education Bill, now before parliament. The 1988 Education Reform Act (ERA), entailed the centrally determined National Curriculum for schools and radical changes to the organisation of education at local authority level, in line with similar changes in the Social and National Health Services. Common features include devolution of financial responsibility and the introduction of a competitive and 'client'-orientated market philosophy. In higher education in general, closely detailed regulation of funding and accountability has proceeded more slowly than in schools but, in teacher education, the regulatory influence of the Department for Education (DFE), (formerly the Department of Education and Science) has long controlled teacher supply, through annual allocation of student numbers and associated funding to each institution in both the former public and private sectors.

For teachers there has been a persistent tension between increasing independence in the running and promotion of schools and greater central control of the curriculum and teacher autonomy. Teacher educators have undergone a corresponding encroachment into their autonomy. In 1984 the DES set up the *Council for the Accreditation of Teacher Education*, CATE, which published a detailed set of content criteria which every initial teacher education course had to be seen to be meeting. These criteria included specified numbers of hours to be spent on certain course elements and a list of topics to be covered in professional education. Standards were to be monitored by CATE, in addition to the normal procedure of external examination. The CATE criteria were modified and extended in *Circular No. 24/89* in 1989, to bring them into line with the Education Reform Act of 1988 and National Curriculum in Schools. These revised criteria introduced the idea of competence outcomes as important standards of professional judgements about student teachers. The range of these competences and the knowledge students are required to 'cover' is vast. Perhaps in recognition of the burden this places upon students and institutions, or perhaps because 'government speak' is purposely vague so as to be flexible, reference to child protection is both oblique and brief:

> Courses should also cover other aspects of the teacher's work, including:
>
> i) the pastoral, contractual, legal and administrative responsibilities of teachers, including the preparation of a teachers to detect the maltreatment of children and an awareness of the health and safety of pupils'(Criterion 6.7).

Criterion 6.7 also contains brief mention of 'developing and sustaining links with parents', 'the significance of links between schools and the wider community' and 'the structure and legal framework of the education service'. There is no mention anywhere of contact or links with colleagues in other, related professions.

The circular also contains a commentary upon the criteria, which is a little less vague and a mite more helpful. It does at least acknowledge the need to know about relevant 'agencies and other facilities':

> Students should understand the nature, purpose and practice of pastoral care, be introduced to basic counselling skills, be ready to undertake the administrative and pastoral duties of a classteacher and be given the opportunity to observe experienced teachers in their contacts with parents. With respect to the maltreatment of children, institutions should consider particularly the guidance issues in DES Circular 4/88.
>
> Students should be made aware of the range of agencies and other facilities with which schools co-operate including social services, police, transport undertakings, health services, school

meals service, school psychological services, youth and community services, sports facilities and museums (Commentary section 6 paras 14/15).

The commentary is just that; it is a gloss *on*, guidance *to* the criteria. It is not part *of* the criteria.

This is the context in which tutors operate when they are involved with planning and implementing both focused professional work and the more broadly-based educational underpinnings of ITE. The externally imposed prescriptions result in vast over-loading for students in terms of the large number of hours per week they are in face-to-face contact with tutors and the high degree of course fragmentation they have to contend with. There is a concomitantly great reluctance to increase either the load itself or its disparity. The issue of child abuse, in all its forms, and the related responsibility of *Child Protection* is seen by both students and staff to be of great importance for teachers and, as such, for student teachers in their programmes of professional development. There were requests from students on the one year Postgraduate Certificate in Education for its inclusion, through the course staff-student liaison committee, in 1990, but there had never been any such request from students following the other type of initial teacher education run by the University of Warwick, the four year (BA with qualified teacher status) degree, until the current academic year, although tutors included child protection in the Infant Variant Course, and in an option on Special Educational Needs, open to junior and secondary phase students, in Year 4.

This apparent lack of demand is interesting in the light of another important characteristic of the context within which this work was undertaken: student maturity. Most of the undergraduates on the four year degree come straight from school at eighteen so are relatively immature and have a relatively narrow experience of the world. Initial Teacher Education is not strong on facilitating development of students' skills in working with other adults, counselling, or coping with stress or trauma, in either themselves or others, of whatever age. The group of PGCE students who requested that the issue be included in their course were, by definition, older and had successfully completed a first degree, at least.

So, to summarise the context: it is one of a very crowded programme, largely controlled and prescribed by the Department for Education and the government-appointed Committee for the Accreditation of Teacher Education, and of predominantly undergraduate, student teachers of about twenty years old and with few opportunities to develop skills of working with other adults in their own or other professions.

Several questions arise from this context:

- How to add child protection to the two ITE courses at the same time as avoiding the displacement of any prescribed elements.

- Whether to deal with the topic by its 'permeation' and attachment to a number of issues or areas already part of the courses, like children and their families, special educational needs in school or personal and social education; or whether to dedicate sessions to child protection.

- How to develop an approach to child protection which is helpful to relatively young and inexperienced undergraduates.

Course inputs were devised bearing in mind two common and broad aims;

i) to develop the student teacher's professional skills and competences;

ii) to raise and analyse issues in primary education in an informed and rational way.

(The order of these aims reflects what will probably be the priorities for Initial Teacher Education by the time this piece is published.)

Two different approaches were taken to implementing these aims in the light of the way the questions listed above related to the two very different routes of initial teacher education: the four year undergraduate degree and the post-graduate certificate in education. Each will be described separately.

The Primary PGCE

This is a thirty seven week course devoted entirely to professional education for teaching. Eighteen weeks are spent in schools working with children and teachers, when students are encouraged to enter into the life of the school and its community as fully as possible. In the final nine weeks students are involved in taking responsibility for a full class of children.

During a busy schedule of preparation to teach across ten areas of the curriculum and five cross-curricular 'dimensions', there is a twelve hour course for consideration of Issues in Primary Education. The issues addressed can, and do, change and the course itself provides an opportunity for students to discuss and explore questions important to them. This provides some contrast to the gathering of information and resources and the development of teaching techniques, which dominate many of the other components of this course.

Three of the eight one and a half hour sessions of this course were devoted to child protection within an educational context. Three professionals were involved: a worker from TACADE; the chief educational social worker from a local county education authority; and an education welfare officer from a nearby metropolitan borough. Our aims were to raise student awareness and knowledge about the role of teachers in the promotion of child protection. As a result of discussion it was decided that: **Week 1** would concentrate on the *broad educational context* of school as a secure and enabling environment, in which a class teacher of young children would show that personal and social education and social education, as well as the academic curriculum, are important. This would link with the day's practical workshop the previous term introducing students to the teacher's role in relation to personal and social education in the primary school. The issue of children disclosing abuse to teachers would be discussed and some ground rules for response laid down, but the emphasis would be on the broad, positive personal relationships between teachers and every child which pervade all good teaching. The person from TACADE would make a short initial presentation and then students would conduct an exploration of TACADE materials for Personal and Social Education through the whole primary curriculum and students' group-derived questions (and of children's disclosure of harm, or 'secrets', if they had not arisen from student questions) would be discussed.

Week 2 would sharpen the focus by defining and explaining the terms *child protection, child physical abuse* and *child sexual abuse* and present information about the main legal framework in which child protection exists — *The Children Act* — and reinforce and develop ground rules for action in school, by consideration of case-study material which concentrated particularly on the issues of *confidentiality* and *significant harm*.

In **Week 3** the EWO, who is involved in in-service work on child protection with teachers in her borough, would examine and develop the case for teacher involvement both to promote child protection and in cases of suspected child abuse. There would be still further reinforcement of ground rules and more opportunities for students to raise questions and anxieties they might have. Examples of child protection policies and procedures adapted by LEAs and individual schools would be examined and discussed.

PGCE outcome and feedback

Attendance and participation were excellent. All three contributors were fulsome in their praise for the students' grasp of information, their willingness to discuss issues, and their recognition of the complexity and potential conflict of protecting both children and civil liberties. The students identified the course and the work on child protection in their evaluations with both PGCE course tutors and external examiners as one of the most useful things they had studied. Its value was seen to be twofold: firstly the legal and procedural information acquired in relation to themselves as teachers and to other professionals and, secondly the confidence they gained by having faced and talked through some aspects of such topics as *child physical and sexual abuse,* and the important professional issues of *confidentiality and disclosure.*

The Four Year Degree (BA (QTS))

One of the great advantages of this route into Qualified Teacher Status is the length of time it gives for student skills, knowledge and philosophy of teaching to mature. Building on this, it was decided to introduce the work in two three hour sessions of a 60 hour course which focuses on young children in families during year two of the degree and to devote one further three hour session to the topic of *child protection* itself, six months later, in year three. This second course includes the study of concepts and problems in primary education within a broader societal context than that of year two.

Work in year two was carried out by a team from the local Law Society, constituted to train both young and experienced lawyers in the content and new thinking/practices associated with the *Children Act.*

The first session was a complex presentation with follow-up questions concerning relevant aspects of the law in relation to children and particularly to the 1989 Children Act. The session was presented by the woman solicitor who leads the training team, a specialist family lawyer and explicitly in favour of both the spirit and letter of changes of the law in favour of children's rights within the

Children Act. In the same week, students were shown a training video, centring on a family dispute.The video enacted the conflict arising from the wish of an estranged father to take his children on a long holiday to the USA, and 'stop-over' with him and his new friend, soon after his daughter gets hurt whilst on an outing with him.

The second three hours comprised a session with a **children's advocate**, who first explained his role under the Act and then gave examples of his job, particularly highlighting how and when he worked with teachers. The students were then presented with scenarios involving all kinds of family situation which, now that the Children Act is operational, could involve teachers. Students were given time between sessions to discuss the situations, their degree of seriousness and the next steps in action, or no action, to be taken. A variety of student views on the situations was canvassed, then evaluated by the child advocate and the solicitor. These two team 'experts' then gave their own assessments of the cases and often argued between themselves about interpretations of the law or the best courses of action. Students were invited, and took up the offer, to contribute throughout.

In the three hours of third year work, the first hour comprised a presentation focusing directly on child protection. This assumed a background knowledge of the Children Act and tackled a variety of issues and questions. These ranged from issues of definition and social meaning attached to such terms as 'abuse' , 'victim' and 'survivor'; to questions about the incidence of physical and sexual abuse of children in families; the role which schools and teachers have played in the past in detection and investigation of such abuse; discussion of the relative reluctance of many headteachers and teachers to become involved; the role of developmental in-service education for teachers. All this was designed to to give them more skills to help children and to prepare them to face up to their own emotional trauma when confronted with possibly abused children, or memories of themselves as victims/survivors of abuse.

The second session consisted of guided, paired role-play centring on a young schoolgirl's revelation of pregnancy to a teacher, and the teacher's reaction. This was followed by extended discussion in groups, where students knew each other very well, but only in the context of professionalism, not of personal matters.

BA (QTS) outcome and feedback

There were two sets of very positive feedback to the second year work The first was from the Law Society team, who praised the ability of students to understand the law itself and the new legal approach to family conflict, crisis and breakdown. What impressed them even more was the maturity and depth of student under-standing of human relationships which they were able to combine with their new knowledge of the Children Act to suggest insightful and practical strategies for resolving problems. Law students and practising solicitors had found it much more difficult to recognise the issues raised by the training video, and their discussion had been less focused and penetrating than that of the student teachers.

Student reaction to these sessions was also positive. They felt engaged and stretched by both the content and the approaches. They considered it important that they be familiar with the Children Act and took seriously the part teachers might play in maintaining family relationships and providing continuity and security for young children at school. They also emphasised how much they welcomed the input and perspective from professionals other than teachers.

In **Year Three**, student feedback was gathered in two ways: the first informal and anecdotal, from group tutors and individual stu-dents, the second by comment invited as an item of a written evaluation of the whole term's course in education. The anecdotal information was very mixed. Some tutors had felt unable to include the follow-up role-play in their sessions because of shortage of time for the course content as a whole, others had developed the role-play discussion at the expense of other work on children's personal and social education, because they considered it important to spend the time on child protection. Yet a third group was besieged by students demanding to discuss the topic itself, and the training of teachers to deal with it, more adequately and at greater length.

Written evaluation by twenty one students fell predominately into the third category. Students were asked to rate the importance of the topic for teachers; to comment on what had been included and how it had been delivered and developed over two years of their course. Most put the work into a 'very important' category. They thought more time and more detailed training were required and that spreading the work over two years was a waste of time. They thought all the sessions in both years had been very useful and had particularly valued the lawyer/social worker sessions, because they gave a multi-professional perspective and one which was not education-centred. All this feedback was immediate (within one week of the third session on child protection) and at the end of the first term of a two term course. A written evaluation of the complete course will be carried out at the end of March. It will be interesting to see if the complete year group of students will have similar or different views when commenting at the end of the course.

Conclusions

Several things emerge clearly. We have managed to avoid displacing any other prescribed element of the courses by introducing child protection as part of an issues course. This component in both BA(QTS) and PGCE courses provides useful flexibility but carries with it also an equivalent degree of danger, in that any topic could be superseded by a strong new claim on time. Work in issues courses has taken the form of specifically 'dedicated' sessions, but an element of 'permeation' was used in the four year degree, when introductory work on the Children Act was subsumed in the broader topic of Children and their Families. It is interesting that the undergraduates had a much stronger reaction to the sessions related to the specific issue of child protection than to the broader-based work on family law.

This reaction relates, also, to the third question, concerning the suitability of the topic for young trainee teachers. All the students from whom we have feedback see the issue of child protection as important for them as teachers to know about and to be able to promote. The PGCE students seemed satisfied with the time devoted to the issues and to the approach adopted in their very crowded and hectic work schedule. BA(QTS) students, on the other hand, wanted more time and emphasis to be laid upon training them to deal with child abuse and to promote child protection in school. Their reaction seemed to be a more emotive and involved one than that of the PGCE students. The reasons for this are not clear. It may be related to maturity (the BA students are some years younger than the graduate students), or a different kind of commitment from students choosing different routes into teaching. Or it may be that the PGCE students evaluated this topic in relation to their course as a whole when they had completed every component and had obtained qualified teacher status whereas the BA students were making immediate judgements after one term in their third year of four.

We shall attempt to make sure that the issue of child protection is included for all students in primary training at the current levels at least. As there has been success with both approaches, we shall retain both for at least one more year, and then look again to see if changes, perhaps to a common approach, might be made. To meet the concern of some students in the BA(QTS) course, it would be possible to put on an option course in the fourth year, providing that the resources could be found. Resources are a real problem for us since we have only one person in the department who could put on such a course, and she is fully committed elsewhere and funds are not easily available to buy in expertise. Another option would be to develop a research project to explore reasons for teachers' seeming reluctant to become involved in child protection and the implications for teachers of the *significant harm* category in the Children Act. An associated teaching programme could be mounted for student teachers to develop their confidence, knowledge and skills in the areas most important for their work in school, which would itself take place under the guidance of an experienced practitioner. We seem to have succeeded in our aim of raising and examining issues surrounding child protection, but have made but a tiny and tentative start on developing associated skills and competences. The question of how far this balance is right for young students engaged in ITE has been raised but not resolved.

Child protection is an issue which throws into sharp relief arguments about rather narrowly instrumental training and a broader education approach to the professional preparation of teachers. It is a true 'issue' relevant to teachers and to the educative process. The end — *protection of children from physical, sexual, and psychological harm* — is readily and universally agreed upon, but the means by which it is to be achieved remains a matter of deep and complex controversy.

References

DES (1984) Circular No. 3/84: *Initial Teacher Training: Approval of Courses* London, HMSO.

DES (1985) *Better Schools*, Cmnd. 9469, London, HMSO.

DES (1988) Circular No. 4/88: *Working Together for the Protection of Children from Abuse: protection within the Education Service*, London, HMSO.

DES (1989) Circular No. 24/89: *Initial Teacher Training: Approval of Courses*, London, HMSO.

HM Government (1988) *The Education Reform Act*, London, HMSO

HM Government (1989) *The Children Act*, London, HMSO

8

Training teachers in child protection: INSET

Dorit Braun and Anne Schonveld

Introduction

Until fairly recently, teachers were not seen as an important target group for child protection training. Yet teachers are the only group of professionals who have daily contact with children so are uniquely placed to detect cases of abuse. Teachers' training and work experience mean that they have knowledge and understanding of child development and of the norms of children's behaviour. They are therefore well placed to notice changes or difficulties in a child's behaviour. Teachers and schools have recognised the importance of seeing children in their family and community context, and have a wealth of background information with which to interpret a child's behaviour. In many cases, teachers develop close and trusting relationships with children, so may be chosen by the child as a trusted person to whom they can disclose abuse. However, it should be noted that there are other people working in schools who might also spot behavioural problems, and to whom children may disclose. These include lunch time supervisors, caretakers, the school secretary, classroom assistants and parent helpers. It may therefore be more appropriate to think about training for whole schools so building on the particular strengths of teachers and school.

In our experience of providing training for teachers and schools we have found that staff often have little confidence about how much they know about child protection issues, and how much they can contribute to child protection in a community. Yet not only do teachers know about child development but schools have also recognised the need to educate the 'whole child' in order to ensure that

91

Link to 5.
& ECM curm?

each child succeeds academically and develops to his or her full potential. Thus, schools recognise the need to address children's social, emotional and psychological needs. Moreover, most people who have chosen to work in schools are motivated by a concern for the welfare of children. So the value base in most schools is very supportive to child protection work. This is a strong basis on which to work.

However, this value base does raise some difficult professional concerns and dilemmas for teachers in relation to child protection. Teachers work hard to develop relationships with children and families, and to base these relationships on trust. This is hard to reconcile with child protection procedures, which require teachers to make a referral without first informing the parents. It is also hard to balance developing mutual trust with teachers' professional obligation to refer cases and their inability to keep child protection disclosures confidential. Teachers are concerned about the damage that invoking the child protection procedures might do to the relationships they have so carefully nurtured. The dilemmas raised by these concerns can be a major block to making a referral, or indeed to taking any action to protect a child. Further blocks to taking action are a lack of good working relationships with other agencies; little knowledge of what might happen to a child and family following a referral; and often a lack of trust of workers in other agencies, combined with ignorance of the roles or constraints of the other professionals involved in child protection.

What should training address?

In our experience, training is the most effective way to overcome the blocks which prevent teachers from making referrals. However, this is only the case if training addresses the specific concerns of teachers and schools, and if staff are given opportunities to work through issues. In other words, it is not enough simply to inform people about the definitions and procedures. Instead, school staffs need opportunities to:

- explore their own feelings, attitudes and values about abuse. This needs to be done with great sensitivity — in any staff there are likely to be survivors of abuse. Feelings, attitudes and values can inhibit people from taking action, so they need to examine what they think abuse is and why it occurs, in order to recognise how their ideas might differ from their professional obligations;

- consider how best to handle a child abuse case. For instance, if a child starts to disclose during a lesson, is there a place where the teacher can take the child to talk? Who will cover the class? If there are concerns but nothing specific, how can all staff be involved in monitoring while also protecting the child's right to confidentiality? These questions need to be considered outside a crisis situation, so that the whole school staff can agree on their internal procedures;

- develop relationships with social services and the police, and increase knowledge of the roles of these agencies in child protection;

- examine the local authority child protection procedures, and work out how to operate them — using case studies of different levels of risk/abuse;

- empathise with the feelings of a child who is attempting to disclose abuse, and develop skills to respond effectively, including how the child and family can be supported after a disclosure, and how staff can be helped to deal with the sensitive and challenging situation when a child returns to school following referral;

- develop skills in relating to parents after a referral has been made, and consider how all parents can be made aware of the school and authority child protection procedures;

- become more familiar with community agencies and resources who can support children, parents, and/or staff, in order to be able to refer people for support;

- examine how child protection issues should be included in the curriculum;

- evaluate the school's child protection policy and further develop it in the light of issues raised by the training.

Practical Issues

It is very helpful if the whole school staff (teaching and non-teaching) can train together — this allows for a shared experience and so for developing a shared understanding of what the school policy and local authority procedures mean in practice in the school.

Schools sometimes expect the designated child protection teacher to provide whole school training, but it is very difficult to run training in one's own establishment, because the 'hidden agendas' are too familiar, and issues of role and status can inhibit a member of staff from taking on the role of facilitator. Therefore, it is helpful to ask outsiders to run the training, but careful thought needs to be given to how outsiders are briefed:

- they need to ensure that materials used will reflect accurately the school's perspective, values and composition;

- they need to leave time to explore feelings, attitudes and values, as these will determine how effective the procedures are in practice;

- they need to provide opportunities for all staff to participate in learning, and to understand the importance of establishing a secure climate, where everyone can contribute and where people can be challenged. This means they need to understand the learning process, and not simply to be able to provide input on child protection issues;

- it is helpful to have two trainers, sothat they can support each other, and so that if anyone is having any difficulties with the course (e.g. a survivor) another trainer is available to talk with them.

Some careful thought needs to be given to time and numbers. Too short a session can simply raise anxieties. People need time to engage in a learning process, rather than to deal superficially with definitions and procedures without a chance to reflect on how these work in practice. Ideally, training works best in groups of up to 20, but this may be incompatible with the desire to train whole staffs of large schools. One way round this is to train a core staff group who can then act as group facilitators on a whole school day.

Dilemmas

The sensitive nature of child abuse, and the possibility that some staff may be survivors — or indeed perpetrators — makes it desirable that people volunteer to take part in training. Yet this may not be compatible with the need for everyone working in a school to receive training. At the least it is important to allow people to opt out of some training activities. Consideration needs to be given to offering support to staff during and after training. This might be available through outside agencies but will need to be checked in advance.

A related difficulty is the issue of confidentiality, regarding both personal and professional matters. The bounds of confidentiality during the training session in relation to discussion about particular families or personal matters, need to be agreed at the beginning. Training which allows participants to explore feelings and values will inevitably raise personal and emotional issues for people, and these need to be handled sensitively, especially when people will continue to work together afterwards.

There are also questions of race and gender which need to be addressed. Men may feel very vulnerable in child protection training, and indeed in their dealings with girls. It may be helpful to allow time for single sex groups to discuss some issues — especially sexual abuse. Equally, as with all training, it is crucial not to ask the 'black' staff to 'represent' their culture and values.

Conclusion

The demanding and difficult nature of child protection training for schools means that trainers need to be confident and sensitive and be able to handle emotive responses and keep the training on track. Schools need to develop confidence about selecting trainers and briefing them on the school's needs, to ensure that the training is appropriate.

Reference

Braun, D. (1988) *Responding to Child Abuse* London, CEDC/Bedford Square Press.

9
Research dilemmas:
No intimacy without reciprocity,
no disclosure without illumination

Carrie Herbert

In April 1986 I began a research project with a group of thirteen fifteen-year old girls from a London comprehensive school. The aim was to discuss with them incidents of sexual harassment they had experienced from male teachers and to find out how they dealt with them. By December of the same year eleven of the girls had disclosed to me the following:

Zohra[1]: Digitally raped at the age of four by a man in the nearby flats.

Carmel: Sexually assaulted at the age of six by a cousin in his house whilst he looked after her for her parents.

Chanel: Approached by a man in a playground when she was six. He took her hand and tried to persuade her into going with him. She managed to run away.

Alex: Raped at age ten by a local shopkeeper.

Zaheda: Forced into playing with her fourteen year old brother's genitals at the age of six.

Collete*: Sexually molested at thirteen by a schoolboy outside her home.

---

* This girl told her mother when it happened.

+ These incidents happened to the girls while I was at the school. Each told me about it within a relatively short time of the attack.

Fitti:	Sexually propositioned at fourteen by a man in the underpass near the school.
Linda:	Chased by men in a car one evening at the age of fourteen; escaped physical harm.
Maria[+]:	Sexually harassed by a boy on a school trip when she was fourteen.
Annmarie[+]	Subjected to an attempted rape at fifteen, wearing school uniform.
Jenny[+]	Sexually assaulted one afternoon by two men in an underpass 300 yards from school, at the age of fifteen.

The questions arising from this catalogue of sexual experiences are many, but the one I want to concentrate on in this chapter is: Why did the girls disclose incidents of child sexual abuse? The answer to this, I believe, lies in the style of the research.

It has been accepted as valid and respectable in ethnographic research communities over the last few generations for ethnographers, who usually came from a particularly narrow and privileged section of the population, to go into communities, usually unlike their own, collect data and then write it up alone in the removed atmosphere of their university rooms. Considering educational ethnographic research alone a plethora of studies was conducted in the seventies and early eighties (Lacy 1970, King 1978, Willis 1978, Ball 1981, Hammersley 1983) in search of information about youth culture in British schools. Before that there had been much ethnographic interest in 'primitive' cultures, researchers going to live with and observe tropical islanders and remote or tribal peoples, then returning to their university base to analyse and write up their findings.

Studies of this nature were problematic for me. They seemed to be based on the notion of the researcher 'going in', interviewing, asking questions, observing and making notes whilst trying to be neutral and objective. I felt that the desire to be neutral and distant was not only misguided but also impossible to achieve. How could researchers clear their minds of instantaneous judgements, avoid selective questioning or stereotypical assumptions? Further, in this research model little was acknowledged of the researcher's background, education, prejudices, political beliefs, what is commonly called 'baggage'. I could find no discussion of issues of intervention, of the possibility and desirability of offering participants alternative perspectives on their situation, nor of attempts by a researcher to provide the researched with a political understanding of significant events.

It was important to my research that intervention, illumination, politics (with a small p) and debate be an integral part of the process, for sexual harassment was a relatively new concept, as well as a phenomenon overlaid with scepticism, ignorance, prejudice, disbelief, ridicule, trivialisation and fear. If I had entered the research site with a questionnaire, a pre-determined interview format, had sat in classrooms watching lessons and then disappeared to write up what I had found, it was likely that no-one would have uttered the term 'sexual harassment', or admitted to having been subjected to it. The crucial elements of human spirit and emotion would be lost in the clinical approach to extracting information. No, the research method needed a more personal, more participant-friendly approach.

I believed that the closer the researcher was to the researched group, especially when dealing with issues of oppression and detriment, the more personal and relevant the data would be. This in turn was more likely to be understood by the researcher if there was the opportunity for both parties to discuss in depth what each meant or, as Elliott states, to 'negotiate meaning.' (Elliott 1980).

So a new research method had to be adopted. The question then was: in what milieu are accounts of sexual abuse, personal invasions of privacy, or experiences of unwanted embarrassing sexual encounters likely to be disclosed?

I can only answer this question in retrospect. The research method I had originally designed to collect examples of sexually harassing moments from the girls included (1) diary writing for all members of the group including me, (2) classroom observation, (3) in-depth individual discussions in the privacy of a small room and (4) whole group round-table discussions on topics associated with the project. The first two strategies for collecting data were abandoned, and it would be fair to say that from mid-May onwards the research was dictated by need rather than by design. However, it is also true that the new data collecting strategies far exceeded my expectations of intimacy with reciprocity, and taught me that with information, or 'illumination' as I call it, comes disclosure.

The research method evolved can be described only with hindsight, rather than from a position of forethought and planning. But rather than describe it from the researcher's point of view, it may be constructive to try and place ourselves in the shoes of a fifteen-year-old girl and wonder what research environment and what conditions would encourage and enable you to talk about unwanted sexual encounters? I shall assume that the researcher is a woman.

You are probably more likely to discuss such issues with a researcher if you like her and if you feel secure about what is happening and if you know what it is she is trying to find out. You are more likely to disclose intimate information if you know she will treat it confidentially, if you have some authority over how your disclosure is used and how it will be analysed, and if you trust her to use it appropriately and sensitively.

If you and she engage in deep conversations in which she relates her experiences and if she takes part in aspects of your life other than the research, if she is available to listen when you have something to say, and you can decide what it is you talk about, if you can ask her questions about herself which she answers sincerely, you are more likely to build up a trusting relationship.

If you see her in public, acting and behaving in a way which is consistent with what she says in private, then you are more likely to expect that what you say to her will be taken seriously and will be believed.

If she gives you information and facts which can help you name and understand the things that have happened to you, so that you know that you are not the only one to whom it has happened and that some of the things you have experienced she has experienced too, then you will feel less of a freak and more of an ordinary person again.

If she keeps reassuring you that what has happened to you was not your fault, that women and girls do not ask for unwanted sexual attention despite what others tell you, that the sexual abuse of children and young people is widespread, and if she tells you that you do have rights, that you don't have to put up with unwanted sexual attention even if people tell you this is normal or too disgusting to talk about, then your changing perception of the world will give you courage to verbalise your feelings about the indignities forced upon you as a young girl.

So I abandoned the research method I originally designed after six weeks when the girls refused to cooperate on two aspects of data collection, namely the diary writing and the classroom observation.[2] A more penetrating, more social, more personal, more participant-friendly and more intimate research method evolved. What principles emerged out of this ad-hoc method, which could be salvaged for use another day? I think there are a several:

- The researcher of intimate violations of women and girls must be a woman, because it is only from the position of a female in this society that one can understand the feeling of powerlessness engendered by sexual oppression at a personal level.

- The researched must want to be involved once the nature and purpose of the project has been explained to them and their advice and ideas must be sought in the data collecting process.

- A private space must be made available and there must be a flexible timetable and long uninterrupted periods together to discuss other things besides the 'topic'.

- The researcher must be in a position to give participants information, or able to illuminate certain issues to help them generalise about their personal situation to enable them to make political connections and understand the concept of sexual oppression.

Beneath these principles are two underpinning beliefs: 'no intimacy without reciprocity' (Oakley 1981) and no disclosures without illumination. The first phrases used by Anne Oakley in a research project in which she interviewed pregnant women, draws to our attention the need for researchers to be seen as people who also have experiences, concerns and questions. Only to take is unfair. To give and take is more just. The second phrase is one which I first used when I realised that it was often after giving a girl some particularly pertinent piece of information, challenging her preconceived ideas, or just answering some factual question honestly, that a disclosure followed. The disclosure did not necessarily happen immediately; in some cases it took two or three weeks before I became aware of the importance of the information I had given.

To illustrate the centrality of these two concepts, let me describe two research conversations I had which illustrate that reciprocity encourages intimacy and how illumination of a topic helps with the construction of knowledge. First a conversation with Zohra poignantly shows how, given particular facts and reciprocal experiences, the young woman was able to put three bits of unconnected evidence together and so to make sense of an intimate violation. The second shows how by challenging Carmel's racist beliefs about rapists, I provided her with some valuable information which she used to make a leap of understanding.

Zohra was a fifteen-year-old Muslim, from a strict and traditional home. Her father didn't let her go out at night, even with female friends; she was not allowed to go to school discos, parties or drama performances, and around the age of thirteen her mother stopped her from going on school trips and overnight field trips. Zohra was resentful about this and talked to me quite openly about her culture's control over its young people. The aspect she was most concerned about was marriage She talked to me often during the first few months of the project about her parents' wish to marry her to a young man from their birthplace. They were suggesting that he come over to London and be married to Zohra regardless of her wishes. Zohra's worry was that there would be an inevitable clash of expectations, experience and language and that this was no basis on which to start a marriage in twentieth century London. She asserted on more than one occasion 'I'm going to marry whoever I want and no-one is going to tell me who I am going to marry. I'm not marrying anyone from (parent's birthplace) because I don't like them. I will marry someone from England who is not my cousin and not a relative. I want someone who is English, who has lived here and knows the way around.'

Over the weeks and months we talked, she would alternate between rebellion and submission over her parents' plan. Then on 8th September Zohra began to tell me about her culture's traditional wedding night and how brides were required to show bloodied sheets. Almost without thinking, I remarked that not all virgins bleed on their first night.

Zohra was astounded by this simple comment and questioned me closely. What continued was a detailed anatomical description of virginity. About ten minutes after this Zohra began to fidget with her hands and wriggle on her seat. She looked uncomfortable (and concerned). I asked her what was wrong. She said nothing, but I pursued this line, asking if she were embarrassed about the questions I asked.

Zohra: No I don't feel anxious, I will answer anything, and I like talking to you, Carrie, because I know you're not going to tell anyone and I feel free to answer. But I don't have any problems. Well, I do have some, but I do tell you about them. I'm not even allowed to tell my cousin some of the things I've told you. So I'm not anxious or nervous, I may seem a bit fidgety, but I'm always like that.

Carrie: Have you got any questions you would like to ask me?

Zohra: (lowering her voice): No.

Carrie: Well some of the girls come in here and ask the most extraordinary questions...

Zohra: Is it hard on the first night, you know, having it, I mean did you ever have it?

Carrie: Well yes, umm.

Zohra: My cousin had it but I haven't asked her how it felt because I want to know how it feels. I'm scared, you know.

I told Zohra about my own personal experience of 'the first time' and also graphically described the physical act of sexual intercourse.

This subject was not discussed again until the 9th November, when at a weekend away from London on a trip organised by the girls and myself, Zohra disclosed that she had been digitally raped at the age of four by a man in a nearby block of flats. She told me that as a result of the information she had gleaned from me, the memories she had of the incident, her understanding about her parents' insistence about her 'not going with boys', and their concern to arrange her marriage soon, she had fathomed the truth of what had happened to her.

Her opening statement to me on that occasion, which though it was not taped I remember distinctly, was: 'I now know that I am not a virgin because of what this man did to me'. The importance of this understanding for Zohra is incalculable. Once she knew what it was that had happened to her and the significance of the digital rape for her in her culture, let alone the emotional trauma, she was in a better position than when she had been living in ignorance and fear.

How a young woman deals with information of this kind and what she does with it is not an easy route either. In this case — and Zohra and I have kept in touch since 1986 — she began to run away from home. She did so on three separate occasions, always with a friend or a sister. They went to a friend's house and stayed away for ten days to three weeks. This happened each time her parents became too restrictive or when the issue of marriage was raised. Finally her parents relented. Now in 1992, Zohra lives at home, has a job in the entertainment industry, and a regular boyfriend who is not of her culture or religion. Her parents have apparently accepted at last that their daughter has different attitudes and have stopped threatening to arrange a marriage for her.

The second girl I want to describe is Carmel. She was a strongly independent young woman from a Muslim country too, although herself a Christian. Her family had to flee their country of origin for political reasons and Carmel often harked back, during our discussions, to the days when she lived in a huge house with servants and chauffeurs and swimming pools.

During one conversation Carmel began to discuss the local newspaper report of yet another rape in the vicinity of the school. She made some racist comments and told me that the men who committed rape were all black, because black people were very angry towards white men and their way of retribution was to rape white women. I was astonished by this assertion and challenged it.

Carrie: Can I tell you a few facts about rape. I am not disputing that there are some black men who feel that way, but the majority of rapist are white men, some married, perfectly sane, quite normal, and the majority of people who are raped, something like 80% are known either well or....

Carmel: (interrupting)... family, that kind of thing?

Carrie: (continuing) casually by the rapist. So only 20% of rapes happen in the streets, in dark alleys...

Carmel: Listen, if I am a multi-millionaire do you think I am scared of being raped? Do you think that would be my main worry? Do you think I am going to walk down an alley, do you think I am not going to take a car?

Carrie: But you can still be raped if you are a female millionaire.. You may get raped by your chauffeur.

Carmel: (Begins talking about her childhood and how she used to take a taxi to school. Says suddenly): I never had to sit down and think, 'what will happen if I get raped?', because it was totally unlikely. But I will tell you that in the kind of condition (sic), to get sexually abused is very likely.

Carrie: By whom?

Carmel: By cousins and that. I think it happened to me, I am not sure. I think I got sexually abused as such, and I think it is going to affect my life.

This disclosure, I argue, happened as a result of the challenge I made with regard to Carmel's two misconceptions: first, her racist belief that all rapists are black and secondly, that rapists are strangers to their victims. The illumination that most rapists 'know' their victim and are often related to them in some way gave Carmel the necessary information to connect with and name an incident of sexual abuse in her life.

In this chapter I have discussed a procedure for collecting data about highly sensitive and personal issues. It is not suitable for all research. It is premised on different values from those normally held by ethnographers. At the heart of this method is reciprocity and illumination. First, reciprocity which allows you the researcher to share your experiences with the research: to tell them that you have been hurt, have submitted and have been subject to unwanted sexual attention. And second, illumination: as a result of your age, experience, education and political beliefs, you are in a position to offer the recipients another window on the world, so that they have information and facts which can empower them to have more autonomy in their lives.

Notes
1   All the names in this chapter are pseudonumns.
2.   A detailed analysis of my research method can be found in *Talking of Silence: the Sexual Harassment of Schoolgirls*, Basingstoke: Falmer Press (1989).

References
Ball, S.J. (1981) *Beachside Comprehensive: a case-study of Secondary Schooling* Cambridge University Press

Elliott, J. (1980) 'Validating case studies' Paper presented at the BERA Conference, Cardiff, September 1980

Hammersley, M. (1983) *The Ethnography of Schooling* Humberside, Nafferton Books

Herbert, C. (1989) *Talking of Silence: the Sexual Harassment of Schoolgirls* Basingstoke, Falmer Press

King, R. (1978) *All Things Bright and Beautiful? A sociological study of infants' classrooms* Chichester, Wiley and Sons

Lacey, C. (1970) *Hightown Grammar* Manchester, Manchester University Press

Oakley, A. (1981) 'Interviewing women: a contradiction in terms' in H.Roberts (Ed) *Doing Feminist Research* London, Routledge and Kegan Paul

Willis, P. (1978) *Learning to Labour* Farnborough, Saxon House

10
Living with uncertainty

Esther Saraga

Introduction

My concerns in this chapter are with 'thinking' and with the desire for 'certainty'. In all the calls for more and better training for social workers and other welfare professionals involved in child protection work, 'thinking' is not an activity that is given a high priority. Such training is likely to focus on the development of particular 'skills' and 'competences' rather than on a critical examination of ideas. Many aspects of current policy and practice are based on a series of assumptions linked by an overall desire for simple technical solutions and for 'certainty'. The failure to think critically about the nature of sexual abuse and about what we do to help means that these assumptions are rarely questioned or tested against theory or evidence.

I want to argue here for the overall importance of critical thinking and also, more specifically, for open debates about different theoretical perspectives on *why* sexual abuse occurs. For whether we are consciously aware of it or not, the explanations we use inform the decisions we make about how to act, at every stage of that intervention. No-one has expressed this more simply and clearly than Sarah Nelson:

> ...decisions on how you deal with each family member depend crucially on how you theorise about them. Is he/she mad, bad, sick or inadequate; blameless, collusive or responsible for the whole thing? Are we looking at a family pathology, a Freudian spiders' web, a legacy of patriarchy?

> Theory decides whether you believe a runaway girl's story... It shapes what you tell the tearful mother... It determines the

policy you design for the offender... It decides whether or not you intervene at all... (Nelson 1987, p97).

However, most current writings on child sexual abuse either ignore the question of why abuse occurs or they take for granted particular explanations, which have as a consequence acquired a status of 'truth'.

Dangerous theory

The desire for certainty can be recognised in several ways. For example, in the desire to 'know' the facts — Did he do it or didn't he? How common is sexual abuse? Who does it? How can we predict or identify abusers? Such questions are asked on the assumption that the 'facts' are, or can be, known, even though research has demonstrated clearly that these facts will depend, among other things, on how abuse is defined and on the methods used in the research, both of which in turn depend upon the theoretical perspective of the researchers (Kelly et al 1991, Saraga 1993). Similarly, when abuse occurs, there is a desire to know 'what went wrong?' and 'who is to blame?', though these questions are rarely concerned with the perpetrator of the abuse. Instead they are asking who failed to protect the child, assuming that protection was possible. Finally there is a desire for simple technical approaches to practice, for clear guidelines which will get it 'right' for children, and protect workers from criticism. The effect of this is that options for action to prevent abuse, to protect children who have been abused, and to help them to recover are closed down. (MacLeod and Saraga 1991).

Recognising that there are different theoretical perspectives means recognising that there may be more than one possible answer to our questions. Therefore one consequence of the desire for certainty is that theory is resisted. Indeed there are in the professional literature, explicit arguments for avoiding theory. For example, theory is seen as leading to debates, and hence conflict:

> The effects of the increasingly public conflicts among the experts resonate powerfully within the multi-disciplinary network, as well as in individual social workers.... the consequences for decision making and the performance of staff are self-evidently harmful to children, parents and workers alike. (Craig et al 1989, p67).

Alternatively, theory is seen as dangerous because it may be applied uncritically and dogmatically:

> There is at present a danger that over-confident, even dogmatic assertions by an exponent of one theoretical position will be seized upon uncritically by social workers who, understandably, crave certainty in an uncertain and stressful area of work. We are not yet at the stage at which such certainties... are sustainable (Stevenson 1989, p 172).

It is interesting that Stevenson's concerns about dogma do not lead her to call for open critical debate of conflicting theoretical positions but, instead, to an avoidance of theory until such time that certainty has been reached. But is 'certainty' of this kind ever possible? The meaning of child sexual abuse is socially constructed; what is considered abusive, and why, has to be understood in a social and historical context, and it will always be contested. A level of uncertainty is therefore inevitable.

I want to suggest a quite different explanation for the avoidance of theory. Asking 'why?' in relation to sexual abuse is seen as dangerous because it raises a set of difficult questions about things we take for granted and in which we have a great deal emotionally invested. These questions are about the nature of the family, parent-child relations and particular gender relations, and they are questions to which there are no simple answers. So the 'rediscovery' of child sexual abuse in the family has challenged fundamental personal beliefs and the ideology of the traditional family as the cornerstone of society. Recognition that 'normal' fathers can be perpetrators of sexual abuse raises doubts about their 'natural' place as head of the family.

> In the domain of child abuse social workers were not only drawing attention to the problems of contemporary family life but were implicitly focusing on men's abuse of power and authority (Jones, 1992, p 50).

Following the guidelines

These concerns about 'what it means for the family' have led to denial of child sexual abuse or, where this is not possible, to attempts to 'contain' the problem within a small set of 'dangerous' or 'dysfunctional' families. (MacLeod and Saraga, 1988, 1991; Saraga 1993). In place of difficult challenges which result from critical thinking and debate, we have, meeting the need for certainty, the guidelines.

> If social workers do their jobs honestly, genuinely putting children's interests above all else, then they will get it right. (Black 1992 p192).

This comment from Robert Black on the events in Orkney and the Inquiry Report from Lord Clyde, expresses the central assumption underlying the government's strategy on child protection. If we can only get the procedures right and train specialist workers in multi-agency teams to follow them, then children can be protected. The focus of all child abuse Inquiries, whether concerned with the 'failure to protect' a child or 'wrongful accusation' of parents, is on 'what went wrong?' and 'who is to blame?', not on whether or why the abuse occurred. And the conclusions drawn are invariably used to strengthen existing guidelines, or to change them, and to call for more or better training for social workers. As Frost and Stein commented in relation to the Beckford Inquiry:

> It becomes almost as if child abuse is caused by lack of communication, missing memos or whatever other problem an inquiry has uncovered (Frost & Stein 1989 p49).

This 'technical' approach to child protection has to be understood in the current political context of social work in general, and of child protection work in particular. Social work can be described as being 'under siege', undergoing radical changes as part of the wider re-structuring of the welfare state (Cochrane 1993).

> British social work is in the midst of its most turbulent period of development since 1945. Faced with an increasingly impoverished client group, and strapped for resources, it has been criticised not only for its failures but for its entire approach (Jones 1992 p43).

Within this broader context, child protection has the highest profile of all social work activities, and is probably synonymous with social work for many people. In the 1980's there were 18 published Inquiry reports into child abuse (DOH 1991) so that:

> at any one time social workers always seemed to be waiting for another inquiry report to be published just as the previous one was being digested. Social work was a profession whose members were continually being forced to reassess their practice (Cochrane 1993 p82).

Workers and agencies are constantly looking over their shoulders for fear of being caught in the media spotlight. It seems as though child protection workers are in a double bind: on the one hand they are seen as specialists, requiring particular training and skills, but on the other hand the work has to be done in the context of ever dwindling resources on the assumption that it can be done, that is, that children can be protected. At the same time, workers' hands are tied in relation to how they can act, and the development of increasingly prescriptive guidelines means that social workers and other professionals can be challenged, including in court, if they do not follow them to the letter.

One of the consequences of the emphasis on getting the procedures correct, and on inter-agency working, is that 'managerial rather than professional skills become more highly valued' (Cochrane 1993 p95). Indeed child protection is invariably described now as a problem to be 'managed' and it has been separated off in training courses and in practice as a distinct activity, separate from 'child care'.

> Social work with children has come to be almost exclusively child protection work.... any sign of a family not coping is almost routinely treated as a case of possible child abuse (Mellon and Clapton 1991 p22).

Although widely accepted and implemented, this managerial approach has not gone uncriticized. For example, some front-line workers have argued that since they are working in a 'risk business' strict policies applicable in every case are not suitable (Neate 1992 p21). A Director of Social Services has even suggested that 'guidelines for the management of abuse are irrelevant and a positive danger... there is no substitute for sound professional practice' (Hawker 1992 p10). However, in voicing their concerns about current policies and practice, few professionals theorise about the nature of sexual abuse. As a result, even though procedures are continually modified or redefined, the assumptions upon which they are based are rarely examined or questioned, nor is it recognised that particular approaches to practice reflect theoretical assumptions about the nature of sexual abuse.

However, if we do start from the premise that 'theory and explanation have a profound impact on practice (because what we do comes from what we 'see', and what we 'see' comes from how we explain') (MacLeod and Saraga 1991 p43), then it is clear that there is another layer of 'certainties' underpinning work in this area, certainties about why abuse occurs. For example, it is commonly assumed that sexual abuse is a 'family problem', despite the fact that research demonstrates that the majority of perpetrators are men who are known to the child, but not necessarily immediate family members.... so that 'focusing on either abuse within the family or by strangers misses the majority of experiences: abuse by a known adult or a peer' Kelly et al 1991 p6). Similarly it is almost invariably accepted without question that abusers are themselves victims of the 'cycle of abuse,' despite the arguments and evidence that challenge this view (Kelly 1992, Saraga 1993). And finally, it is assumed that, as a result of their 'addiction' to abuse, perpetrators require therapeutic treatment rather than punishment

> ... child sexual abusers... are also often themselves a victim of its compulsive and addictive nature. As such sexual abuse is much closer to drug and alcohol addiction than to 'normal' physical child abuse and neglect (King and Trowell 1992 p70).

Statements similar to this appear in the literature wholly unsupported by evidence or a single reference for the reader, as in this case.

Implicit theory

It is important to consider on what basis particular approaches to practice are discussed and criticised. Consider, for example, the tendency automatically to separate children from their family when sexual abuse is suspected, a tendency criticised in the Cleveland Report. Reflecting on the events in Cleveland, Stevenson suggests that the decisions to remove children from their homes

> were not the outcome of measured professional assessment of the risks to a particular child of being left at home. Rather the certain views of some in positions of responsibility, who believed powerfully, and no doubt sincerely, that sexual abuse necessitated separation, created a climate in which others did not feel free or confident to challenge those views. This is understandable given the normal and valid feelings of revulsion which much sexual abuse engenders... it does remind us how dangerously open social workers are both to immediate organisational pressures and to the influence of leaders with strong opinions (Stevenson 1989 p154).

Thus Stevenson suggests that particular strategies and guidelines appear only as the result of powerful beliefs and strong opinions, as if strategies and guidelines are theoretically neutral. Theory only seems to exist if it is made explicit. But if workers are to be defended

against powerful influences and given the tools to challenge domi-
nant views, they need to be able to debate different approaches to
practice, not in a vacuum or by asserting their correctness, but in
terms of the theories that underlie them.

King and Trowell suggest the demand for the removal of children
from their homes is the result of 'the crude, gut response of many to
CSA' (King and Trowell 1992 p68). But it is not inevitable that gut
responses will lead to such demands. This is only the case if, within
the gut feeling, both parents, or the 'family' are being held responsible for the abuse. What is important is that *thinking* helps us to
move away from gut feelings and to argue instead about the explanations for abuse implicit within them. Thus this view is associated
with orthodox professional accounts that explain abuse in terms of
dangerous *families*, and which also hold mothers responsible for
'colluding' or 'failing to protect her child'. It follows logically that, if
the whole family is dangerous, then removal of the child is the best
option. Such an argument does not have to be made explicitly; it is
implied every time authors refer to 'sexually abusing/abusive
families' or to 'sexually abused families' (See e.g. Fawcett 1989,
Masson & O'Byrne 1990), and in the extraordinary way in which
most writing on this subject, including the Cleveland Report, refers
all the time 'to parents' rather than to 'mothers' and 'fathers', even
though in the overwhelming majority of cases the man is the suspected perpetrator.

> Suddenly a world that is completely unapologetic about using
> masculine pronouns as generic terms, studiously avoids them,
> showing a remarkable reluctance to attach a gender to an
> abuser (MacLeod and Saraga 1991 p35).

An alternative view on child sexual abuse, which holds the abuser
responsible, is likely to be associated with gut feelings that focus on
the abuser. This approach leads to calls for the abuser to be removed,
and it derives from a different theoretical perspective — feminism
— which puts gender as a central factor in understanding why
sexual abuse occurs (MacLeod and Saraga 1988, 91; *Feminist Review*
1988; Driver & Droisen 1989). It is important to recognise the theoretical conflict here, because discussion of 'parents' in official Inquiries,
in guidelines and in the Children Act reduces the possibility of
developing an alternative practice based on a different set of explanations.

By deconstructing 'parents' into mothers and fathers, a feminist perspective leads to a different practice which recognises that a non-abusing partner, usually a mother, is not responsible for the abuse, even though she may react to the news with anger or denial. This approach seeks to support the mother, both in her own right, and for her to be more able to believe and support her child. Thus this alternative practice does not guarantee that children can stay in the non-abusing part of their family, but it *increases the probability*. It is derived from a feminist analysis of the causes of sexual abuse and backed up by research evidence and the personal testimony of survivors, which demonstrates that being believed by their mothers at the time of the disclosure of abuse or later was a crucial part of the process of recovery (See MacLeod and Saraga 1991 for further discussion). In presenting this alternative approach, I am not arguing against a framework of procedures nor for simply replacing one set of rigid procedures with another but for a different way of thinking about how to proceed.

Prescriptive procedures make it harder for workers to think about and therefore take account of the whole of a child's circumstances. In order to help children it is necessary to understand the *meanings* abuse has for them, for the abusers, for non-abusing parents, for relatives and for workers; to consider how these meanings may vary with personal and social circumstances, how they are affected by gender, 'race', cultural difference, class, sexuality and disability, and how they might determine the options available for helping. There is a danger that the desire for certainty will lead to the development of another set of rules about, say, the gender or 'race' of workers who should work with particular children. But such rules are not at all helpful since they deny individual experiences.

> Though we cannot, indeed must not make definite predictions about their impact on people, we need to be alive to all the possibilities without limiting the options we make available to people on the basis of our assumptions about the choices they feel are open to them (MacLeod and Saraga 1991 p42).

The dominance of the law

Another assumption of current practices is the belief that the law can, and should be, the ultimate arbiter of the truth.

> One of the services that the law performs is to transform complex messy situations.. into a simple story which makes

sense and holds a moral for everyone. To go behind court judgements... to start doubting the law's version of the truth would raise serious problems... (King and Trowell 1991 p1-2).

Although the introduction of new legal guidelines is always accompanied by caveats about acting 'in the best interests of the child', it is rarely acknowledged that those 'best interests' are generally also a matter for interpretation and judgement.

We listen to what children tell us and we try to take a critical approach to the meanings we invoke for what they say. Of course, children's needs and rights must be put first. But it is not a simple matter to know what children's needs are in the long or the short term. Even less is it easy to produce the correct strategies through which to intervene to meet their need; if only it were (MacLeod and Saraga 1991 p32).

Consider, for example, the criticism of social workers in the Orkney 'crisis' for asking 'leading questions', a criticism that led to calls for better training for specialist social workers to learn how to conduct an investigation without 'contaminating the evidence'. Is it possible that the legal requirements for evidence may be incompatible with the therapeutic value for children of naming their experiences? How do we weigh up these two 'needs'? Can such questions even be raised?

It is encouraging to see that increasingly welfare professionals are expressing concern about the domination of child protection work by legal processes. For example, discussing the Home Office guidelines for interviewing children on video, Wattam suggests that 'balancing the needs of justice and the needs of children will be difficult' (Wattam 1992 p.7). More generally, and very cogently, King and Trowell argue: 'In cases involving children's welfare there is a high price to be paid for using the law to protect individual and family rights in this way' (King and Trowell 1992 p2). The demand for investigations to provide evidence that can be used in a criminal court may in some instances not be in the best interests of the child

After the 'discovery' of child sexual abuse, any clinical interview with children becomes potential evidence for legal action any hint of sexual abuse means that *all normal therapeutic procedures must end* (King and Trowell 1992 p71, my emphasis).

They point out that there is a clinical justification provided for this procedure: 'that it will probably be much better for the child to have the disclosure in the form of a video recording....than to subject the child to repeated interviews' (p71). But what is meant by 'better' in this context? And who has decided this, on what basis and on what evidence? Clearly there is a very important debate to be had here, since, as King and Trowell suggest, 'closing an interview or changing its style may be extremely disruptive to children' (p71).

The failure to question guidelines and procedures, to ask *why* they are as they are, means that few people have challenged this central tenet of practice, that therapeutic work with children must await the completion of legal processes. Yet, as King and Trowell point out: it does not have to be like this. Other countries (e.g. France and Holland) 'have succeeded in separating the investigative role from the therapeutic role' (King and Trowell, p132).

Thinking about feelings

Despite the emphasis on following guidelines, it is recognised in both training and supervision that child protection work raises painful and difficult feelings in workers. However it is usually only certain kinds of feelings that are acknowledged, and workers are rarely encouraged to *think* about the nature of their feelings and how analysis of them might give them further insights. So, for example, when a child is abused within the family, it is common for workers, as well as for children (and their mothers themselves), to feel that in some way their 'mother' is also to blame or that she *must* have known. Such feelings can not only be acknowledged or expressed, they can also be analysed to consider why they are so widespread. They can be understood in terms of an analysis of the role of 'mothers' in society, of the ideology of motherhood, of the expecta-tions that we all have or had of our own mothers, and of the fear that if it is possible 'not to know', then this could happen to our own children. This kind of analysis can help workers to separate off these common *feelings* from their *thinking* about what has happened and to act on the basis of the latter rather than the former. They are also in a position to help others to understand the nature of these feelings. As Mary MacLeod always says in training: 'Feeling to blame is not the same as being to blame; and feeling not to blame is not the same as being not to blame'.

Similarly when the impact of a worker's 'personal business' on their role as a professional and their capacity to manage the work is discussed, it is generally the impact of (usually) her own abuse in childhood that is considered. The impact of having abused or harassed is rarely mentioned. And when debating the role of male workers in child sexual abuse work, the discussion usually focuses on whether the child will feel 're-abused' by a man (Harris 1990 p.9). But the impact of gender on individual workers and on the dynamics between workers is much more complicated than either of these two examples would suggest, and it can only be understood by reference to a theory which recognises the links between child sexual abuse and other forms of male violence against women and children.

> An explanation that takes account of gender enables us to acknowledge that men and women have very different relationships with this issue.... if we are women is our business to deny our anger or to vent it? To abuse the perpetrator or to defend him? To protect ourselves from anxiety about our children and the men we love, or to expose every abuser? For men, can we listen to anger at abusers and men or is our business to prove that we are not abusers? Is this our vehicle for the expression of violent feelings by proxy? (MacLeod and Saraga 1991 p42-43).

Analysis of personal emotions and of interpersonal dynamics in the context of a feminist understanding of the causes of abuse can help both women and men to be more confident that they are focusing on the child's business and not their own. And this is likely to be of much greater value to children that any of the current debates about whether men should or should not do this work.

Protection or prevention?

In this chapter I have argued that far from undermining certainty, theory and debate can help us both to live with and benefit from the uncertainty, in particular by providing a way of comparing and arguing about different approaches to practice.

> Consensus may be comfortable, but without criticism and debate we lose opportunities to see things differently, and to work differently. There is no place for an embargo on debate within the public response to child abuse; nor need we be apologetic about disagreements; they have frequently led to new insights (MacLeod and Saraga 1991 p32).

It is only by asking fundamental questions about why abuse occurs that we can move away from the singular focus on child *protection* to real *prevention* of abuse.

Ignoring the underlying causes of abuse leads to the implicit assumption that abuse will always be with us. Consider for example the ideas of Cashman and Labelle-Armstrong, members of the community group 'Cleveland against Child Abuse'. Recognising the importance of considering child sexual abuse as a social problem, moving away from the focus on individual children, they suggest that abuse is 'endemic in society' and argue therefore for local and national policies geared towards creating the 'ideal', 'child-loving society':

> Imagine a society which cared enough for its children to protect them from sexual abuse... the elements of a child protective society therefore would include awareness of the problem, provision of help for abusers or potential abusers, and the encouragement of assertiveness with children (Cashman and Lambelle-Armstrong 1992 p120).

It is depressing to note that even though they are describing an ideal society, abuse will still occur. I wonder why it did not seem possible to write 'imagine society in which children are not abused'? Other writers similarly assume that abuse is inevitable but do not even aspire to the protective society described by Cashman and Lambelle-Armstrong. Dingwall asks: 'Would it not be better if we could prevent children from ever being harmed?' (1989, p49). But his answer is formulated not in terms of the prevention of abuse but of the protection of children: 'It is not clear that a free society would ever tolerate the sort of surveillance that would be necessary to provide such a guarantee' (Dingwall 1989 p49).

Neither Cashman and Lambelle-Armstrong nor Dingwall examine the theoretical assumptions upon which their views are based. How we help abusers, for example, will depend upon our explanation for why they have abused. Of course, there are no easy answers to understanding why abuse occurs and therefore no easy ways of stopping. it. But if we do not even start from the ideal of preventing abuse, rather than protecting children, we lose opportunities for developing explanations and therefore limit our options for helping. More generally, I have suggested that we have to be prepared to accept the many levels of uncertainty that exist in this area of work. Open discussion and debate of different theoretical approaches can help us to live with this uncertainty and make real progress in understanding and practice.

References

Black, R. (1992) *Orkney: A Place of Safety?* Edinburgh, Canongate Press.

Cashman, H. & Lambelle Armstrong, A. (1991) 'The Unwanted Message: Child Protection through Community Awareness' in Richardson, S. & Bacon, H. (eds) *Child Sexual Abuse: Whose Problem?* Birmingham, Venture Press.

Cochrane, A. (1993) 'Challenges from the centre' in Clarke, J. (ed) *A Crisis in Care? Challenges to social work*, London, Sage.

Craig, E, Erooga, M. Morrison, T. & Shearer, E. (1989) 'Making sense of sexual abuse — charting the shifting sands' in Wattam, C., Hughes, J. & Blagg, H. (eds) *Child Sexual Abuse* Harlow, Longman.

Department of Health (1991) *Child Abuse. A Study of Inquiry Reports 1980-89*, London, HMSO.

Dingwall, R. (1989) 'Some problems about predicting child abuse and neglect' in Stevenson, O. (ed) *Child Abuse,.* London, Harvester Wheatsheaf.

Driver, E. & Droisen, A. (eds) *Child Sexual Abuse*, London, MacMillan.

Fawcett, J. (1989) *Breaking the Habit: the Need for a Comprehensive Long-Term Treatment for Sexually Abusing Families*, Occasional Paper Series 7, London, NSPCC.

Feminist Review (1988) 'Family Secrets: Child Sexual Abuse' *Feminist Review*, 28.

Frost, N. & Stein, M. (1989) *The Politics of Child Welfare*, London, Harvester Wheatsheaf.

Harris, J. (1990) 'Sexual abuse: counsel of despair to ban male staff working alone with women', letter in *Community Care* 22nd November, 9.

Hawker, M. (1992) 'Abuse guidelines 'a danger' letter in *Community Care* 11th June, 10.

Jones, C. (1992) 'Social work in Great Britain: Surviving the Challenge of Conservative Ideology' in Hokenstad, M.C., Khinduka, S.K. & Midgley, J. (eds) *Profiles in International Social Work*, Washington, DC, NASW Press.

Kelly, L. (1992) *'Outrageous injustice'* Community Care Inside Supplement, 25th June, ii.

Kelly, L., Regan, L. & Burton, S. (1991) *An Exploratory Study of the Prevalence of Sexual Abuse in a Sample of 16-21 year olds*, Child Abuse Studies Unit, Polytechnic of North London.

King, M. & Trowell, J. (1992) *Children's Welfare and the Law*, London, Sage.

MacLeod, M. & Saraga, E. (1988) 'Challenging the orthodoxy: towards a feminist theory and practice', *Feminist Review* 28.

MacLeod, M. & Saraga, E. (1991) 'Clearing a path through the undergrowth: a feminist reading of recent literature on child sexual abuse.' in Carter, P., Jeffs, T. & Smith, M.K. (eds) *Social Work and Social Welfare Yearbook 3*, Milton Keynes, Open University Press.

Masson, H. & O'Byrne, P. 'The Family systems approach: a help or hindrance?' in The Violence against Children Study Group (eds) *Taking Child Abuse Seriously*, London, Unwin Hyman.

Mellon, M. & Clapton, G. (1991) 'Who are we protecting?' *Community Care*, 7th March, 22.

Neate, P. (1992) 'In the face of adversity' *Community Care*, 29th October, 20-22.

Nelson, S. (1987) *Incest: Fact and Myth*, Edinburgh, Stramullion Press.

Saraga, E. (1993) 'The abuse of children' in Dallos, R. & McLaughlin, E. (eds) *Social Problems and the Family*, London, Sage.

Stevenson, O. (1989) 'Reflections on social work practice' in Stevenson, O. (ed) *Child Abuse*, London, Harvester Wheatsheaf.

Wattam, C. (1992) 'For justice and therapy?' *Community Care* 27th August 1992, 7.